Self-Coaching with

WILLEM LAMMERS

SELF-COACHING WITH LOGOSYNTHESIS

How the power of words can change your life

Copyright ©Willem Lammers, 2015
Institute for Logosynthesis®
Pardellgasse 8a, CH-7304 Maienfeld.
www.logosynthesis.net, info@logosynthesis.net

Translated by Ashley Werner

1st edition, 2015
All rights reserved – most notably those of reproduction, distribution and translation.

Logosynthesis® and translations of this term are registered trademarks of the author, Willem Lammers, and may not be used without his express prior consent.
Please read the disclaimer on page 192 before reading this book and applying the techniques that it presents.

Clients' names and personal information have been changed.

ISBN-13: 978-1505825909
ISBN-10: 1505825903
Cover design: Diana Wesley
Typesetting: Ruby Door Art & Design
Printing: CreateSpace

For Andrea

Contents

Preface: amazement   9

I Developing as people
1. How it all began — 13
2. Learning pathways — 15
3. Self-coaching: an example — 17

II Understanding Logosynthesis
4. Why your true Self doesn't suffer — 25
5. How your being can break apart — 35
6. How energy freezes in space — 49
7. How words work miracles — 57
8. How we dissolve structures — 63
9. How Tony suppresses a memory — 67
10. Understanding the brain — 73

III Learning Logosynthesis
11. Clear a space — 77
12. Zoom in on the suffering — 85
13. Examine the triggers — 89
14. Say the sentences — 97
15. Allow the words to take effect — 103
16. Reassess the topic — 113
17. Shape the future — 119

IV Applying Logosynthesis

18	Dissolving fear	125
19	Overcoming shame	133
20	Processing grief	139
21	From anger to forgiveness	145
22	Unleashing love	151
23	Revitalising the body	161
24	Kicking habits	171
25	Dismantling beliefs	177

V In conclusion

Bibliography   189

About the author   191

Preface: amazement

Our learning pathway

We learn throughout our lives. We develop – physically, mentally and spiritually. We grow up, get older, and our physical strength decreases. Our path continues onwards, always offering new opportunities, challenges and obstacles. We either receive help from others or have to rely on ourselves. The path is never smooth or straight. It may appear straight from time to time, but we never avoid meeting our destinies via the unexpected.

I spent many years searching for the nature of change and development in humans as a psychotherapist, coach and someone with an interest in spiritual affairs. After countless hours of training, coaching and psychotherapy, a minor miracle finally appeared before me: the miracle of words. The miracle led to a coherent system for personal and professional development. I called this system Logosynthesis. I was able to assemble the individual puzzle pieces of my experience into a fascinating overview. Principles of development and change gradually slotted together with the origin of our experience as humans.

Phrases to freedom

Logosynthesis is a pioneering new model for guided change. It helps in the influencing of physical, emotional and mental states with the assistance of an unusual principle: the power of words. Logosynthesis offers an elegant and versatile model along with a surprisingly effective method.

I wrote the first book about the self-application of Logosynthesis for my clients in 2008. I've since continued to develop Logosynthesis at a rapid pace. This book takes you right up to the cutting edge. It'll help you to solve your everyday problems and tackle a variety of issues, including:

- Recognising and achieving your goals in life
- Assuming control over your life
- Shaping your relationships in a vibrant and positive manner
- Releasing time and energy so that you're able to enjoy your existence
- Increasing your performance, efficiency and satisfaction at work.

I'd like to take this opportunity to thank the many people who have made a contribution to this book. The most important among them are Andrea Fredi, Rudolf Karlen, Jürg Kesselring, Ursula Marti, Ulrike Scheuermann and Karin de Smit. Special thanks also go to Diana Wesley for the cover, Stacey Grainger for the layout, and Ashley Werner, without whom the book would have been published much later (if ever!).

Free yourself from the burden of old memories and frozen patterns of thought, feeling and behaviour. Follow your inner voice – the voice of your Essence, your higher Self.

Maienfeld, Switzerland, Autumn 2014.

Willem Lammers

PART I
DEVELOPING AS PEOPLE

1 How it all began

Leonore – 'Living beside her shoes'

LOGOSYNTHESIS CAME INTO BEING ON 11 JANUARY 2005. It was then that I had a consultation with Leonore, a small and unsettled woman who was around 45 years old. Leonore had fallen down a flight of stairs in a railway station some six years ago and had been frightened, sad and disoriented ever since. She couldn't remember exactly what had happened on that day in the station. All she knew was that she'd been trying to board a train and that the fall, however it had occurred, had caused her harm.

During our session, Leonore said, "I'm living beside my shoes." This Swiss German expression means 'I'm crazy.' It sounded as if she perceived herself and her physical body as being in different places. She backed up my hypothesis by telling me how she'd struggled with her shower cubicle door that very morning. She'd reached out for it but had missed; her hand hadn't gone where she'd wanted it to go. As she talked, I noticed her shadow begin to flicker in the sunlight to her right. I was surprised at the combination of signals, so I decided to take her up on her choice of phrase. I shared my thoughts and asked if she could bring the two parts of herself together. She was scared by the prospect, but she agreed to try once I'd reassured her that she could stop the experiment at any time.

Leonore imagined the two parts of herself sliding into one another. Intense feelings soon surfaced and she started to tremble and cry – but after around ten minutes she was able to tell me exactly what had happened in the train station on that fateful morning six years ago. It turned out that someone had hurried past her on the stairs, knocking her over and leaving her unconscious on the cold concrete floor. She was completely disoriented when she came around, and she walked about for hours before she was eventually able to call her husband to pick her up and take her home. After this incident, nothing had been the same for her again.

The development of Logosynthesis

The session with Leonore made a powerful impression on me. I began to examine her and other people's stories more closely. I discovered that the splitting of the Self into different parts isn't the exception, but rather the rule. I found out that we exist within personal energy fields and that these spaces are often set up like museums, filled with statues of people from our past and fantasies about our future. We tend to react to these statues and fantasies as if they were real. In fact, the objects in our personal spaces distort the perception of our environment in the here-and-now, and they do this with far-reaching consequences.

I was fascinated by these discoveries and slowly learned to understand what had initially caused me so much surprise. I also discovered how people can piece together their split parts and clear out their personal museums. We can actually leave behind the burdens of both our memories of the past and our fantasies about the future. We can then begin to live in the here-and-now without permanently and painfully confronting or suppressing our life stories. The power of words is what makes this possible; special sentences are said and then allowed to take effect.

I continued my research as part of my work as a companion to people in their development. My observations, experiences and reflections ultimately produced a coherent system for coaching and development. I called this system Logosynthesis: 'bringing together with words'. Many of my counselling, coaching and psychotherapy colleagues in both Europe and overseas have since come to know and appreciate Logosynthesis.

I published my first book on the subject in 2007 as *Change through the Magic of Words*. This title is an introduction to Logosynthesis for coaches, counsellors, supervisors and psychotherapists. The first book about self-coaching with Logosynthesis followed in 2008 as *Phrases to Freedom*.

Logosynthesis has continued to develop, and more and more people are now using the system for their personal and spiritual development. In the following pages I'll show you what Logosynthesis is and how you can use it for yourself. Welcome to the world behind the mirror!

2 Learning pathways

> Everything flows, nothings stays still.
>
> HERACLITUS

THIS BOOK INTRODUCES THE SELF-APPLICATION OF LOGOSYNTHESIS. It won't provide answers to all of your questions and it won't render professional support redundant. In some stages of life it's simply better to place your trust in the care, experience and competence of a trained professional. Coaching and psychotherapy apply Logosynthesis in a much deeper way than it's possible to cover in these pages. Professionals can learn about applying Logosynthesis in this deeper way by attending sessions with Logosynthesis trainers.

Your Self is the best coach

This book will teach you how to use Logosynthesis for self-coaching. In other words, you'll learn how to be coached by your Self. Your real Self, your Essence, is the best coach you'll ever have. Why? Because with this coach you'll:

- Always have a clear purpose
- Pursue this purpose courageously and without compromise
- Be excellent at interacting with people and respecting their capabilities and limits

- Correctly assess your own capabilities and limits and be able to set priorities
- Know which skills to use in any given moment
- Always have full access to all of your knowledge
- Recognise your emotions as an early warning system for risks and opportunities
- Know when you need help
- Not be alone but also not depend on other people
- Be willing and able to learn.

A coach like this would be invaluable in the business world, but you already have him (or her!) – and he's always there for you. Logosynthesis helps you to discover this coach within yourself and engage his services on a permanent basis. You can call on him whenever you want, and with time you may no longer want to do without his support. You'll get valuable assistance with your everyday challenges by using him regularly. You'll find it much easier to recognise and realise your goals in life.

Liberate yourself – your real Self – from difficult memories, emotional wounds, limiting beliefs and restrictive ideas. You won't be able to resolve everything today, but you'll certainly be able to make a start.

3 Self-coaching: an example

> Reality isn't what I'd like it to be.
> It isn't what it should be.
> It isn't what people told me it was.
> It isn't what it once was.
> Nor is it what it'll be tomorrow.
> The reality around me is simply what it is.
>
> JORGE BUCAY

Cleo's self-coaching

THIS CHAPTER GIVES YOU AN IDEA OF WHAT THE APPLICATION OF LOGOSYNTHESIS IS ABOUT. It uses the example of Cleo and her boss. You'll see how Cleo is able to use Logosynthesis to dissolve her fear and neutralise its triggers.

Cleo meets her boss

Cleo is a 26 year-old marketing assistant. She's worked at her current company for two years and loves her job even though it's often very challenging. One morning she receives an email from her boss, Mark, inviting her to an urgent meeting next Friday. He doesn't include any further explanation. Cleo begins to feel uneasy as she reads the email. She can't concentrate on her normal tasks over the next few hours. Her head is full of images of Mark shouting at her or even firing her. She notices an opportunity for applying Logosynthesis when she realises that this game of mental make-believe is going on. She learnt about Logosynthesis in a workshop a short while ago. She prepares a glass of water, disconnects the telephone, and settles down to focus on the problem. She starts to explore the issue by posing the following questions:

- *What's happening in my body?*
- *What emotions have been triggered?*
- *What thoughts are going through my head?*
- *How distressed am I by all of this on a scale from 0 to 10?*

Cleo now notices some signs of tension in her body – a lump in her throat, a tight feeling in her stomach and a pulling sensation in her shoulders. There are emotions bound up in this tension; she notices fear, shame and some slight anger. Thoughts begin to emerge that she's incompetent and not up to her job. But she also thinks that her boss needs to give her more direction.

All of these physical feelings, emotions and thoughts are associated with considerable stress. When she thinks about next Friday, she rates her level of distress as an 8 on the scale from 0 to 10.

When Cleo examines this distress, she realises that the physical symptoms, emotions and thoughts must be reactions to a fantasy construct. She now examines exactly what has led to her considerable distress. She investigates her ideas about the upcoming meeting and concentrates on her worst vision – that Mark will shout at her and say that the company no longer requires her services. She asks herself more questions:

- *Who or what is most significant in this fantasy?*

In this case it's clearly Mark, her boss.

- *Where in the space around myself do I perceive him?*

In her vision, Mark is directly in front of her, about two metres away.

- *How do I know that he's there? Can I see, hear or feel him?*

Cleo can see an image of her boss's reddened face, hear him yelling loudly and feel a crushing wave of energy.

She's learnt that these sights, sounds and feelings can trigger distressing physical and emotional reactions. She now knows enough to apply Logosynthesis, so she works out the first sentence. This sentence retrieves all of her energy that's bound up in the images, sounds and other sensory perceptions that are part of her fantasy of being fired:

I retrieve all my energy bound up in the representation of Mark firing me and take it back to the right place in my Self.

Cleo says the sentence aloud in a calm voice and without any particular emphasis. She then pauses to allow the words to take effect. She only observes during this pause, just as if she were watching clouds pass by in the sky. Once some 30 or 40 seconds have passed, she notices that something has changed and that she's relaxed. She carries on with the second sentence:

I remove all non-me energy related to the representation of Mark firing me from all of my cells, from my body and from my personal space, and I send it to where it truly belongs.

She allows the sentence to take effect again. She watches what happens inside herself. A minute passes and she notices how deeply she's breathing and how her shoulders have relaxed. The lump in her throat has disappeared and she begins to feel very calm. She now drafts the third sentence. This sentence retrieves all of her energy that's bound up in her reactions to the imaginary scene:

I retrieve all my energy bound up in all my reactions to this representation of Mark firing me and take it back to the right place in my Self.

Cleo pauses yet again and observes while the third sentence's words do their work. This takes around a minute. She's now relaxed, her stomach doesn't feel tight, and she can feel her life energy flowing back into herself. She compares this new state with how she felt before she said the sentences.

Something interesting has happened: Cleo suddenly sees the world through different eyes. Her fear of her boss has dissolved and her desire to avoid him has disappeared. Cleo realises that Mark is just a stressed manager who's overwhelmed with his responsibility. He actually needs her help to carry his burden. She needs to make clear to him how she wants to be led; Mark definitely can't read her mind.

Cleo is now reassured and knows how to prepare for the meeting. She drinks a glass of water and continues with her work. The meeting on Friday will be a perfect opportunity to set out a new arrangement with her boss.

Applying Logosynthesis helped Cleo to transform inappropriate reactions into a state of competence and satisfaction. Before she was fearful, tense and confused, but she's now able to understand Mark's perspective and reconcile this perspective with her own. She recognises her own responsibility in their cooperation.

What does Cleo do to dissolve her fear?

This is a typical application of Logosynthesis in self-coaching. Mark's invitation confronts Cleo with a challenge that she feels unable to deal with. Her fantasy of the meeting leads to unpleasant physical feelings, emotions and thoughts. On closer examination it turns out that these reactions are actually triggered by fantasies of what might occur. Cleo isn't looking for the triggers of these fantasies in her past when she applies Logosynthesis; she remains in her current awareness. You'll learn about deeper levels of application later in this book.

Cleo passes through the following stages as she deals with her issue:

- She subconsciously constructs a fantasy video of how the meeting with Mark might turn out
- She reacts to this fantasy with limiting thoughts, distressing emotions and painful physical sensations.

The Logosynthesis workshop taught Cleo to examine and scrutinise her own processes. During her self-coaching, she realises that she's creating fantasy images and then reacting to these images with distressing physical feelings, emotions and thoughts. She investigates both these reactions and the fantasies that triggered these reactions. She then says three specific sentences and leaves a pause after each one. She watches closely for what happens during these pauses. Saying the sentences aloud immediately changes Cleo's thoughts, emotions and physical sensations; the images become neutral and she's able to think, feel and act in a different way. The meeting with Mark now offers an opportunity to redefine their collaboration.

Such a sequence of events is common when Logosynthesis is applied, much to the astonishment of everyone involved. I've worked with Logosynthesis in my professional and private life for many years, but even now I'm constantly surprised at the sentences' effects. Even people who have only read a simple introduction to the model can have incredible reactions, just like one of my colleagues reported:

I'd really like to meet other people who have discovered the fantastic effect of Logosynthesis in their work. My enthusiasm just won't stop growing. I've seen incredibly good results in my own small circle – with my daughter, my friends, my brother and recently also my boyfriend. Everyone notices the effect straight away. People who come into the house crying leave with smiles on their faces. I can barely wait for the course in September.

Are you curious to find out more?

PART II

UNDERSTANDING LOGOSYNTHESIS

It's up to you: theory or practice?

WHAT FOLLOWS IS A DETAILED SECTION ON LOGOSYNTHESIS' BACKGROUND AND PRINCIPLES. You now have two options:

1. Do you want to understand Logosynthesis before you start out with the practical application? I'd like to invite you to read this section if that's the case. This is where I cover Logosynthesis' principles and how I discovered them. There are also some exercises that help you to understand the theory in both intellectual and much broader terms. You'll end up with a solid understanding of the theory behind your own Logosynthesis applications.

2   Do you prefer to learn in a more hands-on manner? Would you like to start experimenting with the model straight away? If this is the case, I suggest that you skip this chapter and move onto Section III. This is where I initiate you into the secrets of how Logosynthesis is applied. It won't be long before you're gathering your own set of surprising experiences. You can always return to Part II later on to compare the theory with what you've encountered.

Be prepared for something new whether you choose to begin with the theory or the practice. Logosynthesis' principles and methods are very distant from the conventional, materialistic view of the world. This often makes them seem strange and even unbelievable to many readers. Brace yourself for a surprise!

4 Why your true Self doesn't suffer

> When you're inspired by some great purpose, some
> extraordinary project, all of your thoughts break
> their bonds. Dormant forces, faculties and talents become
> alive and you discover yourself to be a greater
> person by far than you ever dreamed yourself to be.
>
> -- PATANJALI

The first principle of Logosynthesis

Our true Self doesn't suffer. We suffer because the awareness of our Essence is lost.

IN LOGOSYNTHESIS, WE'RE MORE THAN A PHYSICAL BODY THAT ENDEAVOURS TO SURVIVE ON EARTH AND PASS ON ITS GENES. We're more than a mind that consciously tries to achieve its goals in this world. We're more than nature and nurture: we're Essence, a Higher Self beyond life on Earth. But we're often unaware of this Essence and many of us have lost contact with it. The following exercise will bring you somewhat closer to awareness of your Essence.

EXERCISE: EVERYTHING MAKES SENSE...

Find a quiet place and relax. Start breathing in and out deeply. As you exhale, softly say the word 'Relax' until a deep sense of relaxation permeates your limbs...

Imagine yourself going back in time... Remember a situation or moment in which your entire life energy was available and you had the feeling that 'Yes, everything makes sense...' Retrieve this situation in your consciousness along with its associated thoughts, emotions and bodily sensations. Examine the situation further:

- *When was it?*
- *Where was it?*
- *Who was there?*
- *How did you feel in your body?*
- *What emotions did you perceive?*

Write down your answers and compare them with the following answers that were given by a seminar group:

- *We danced and were in love*
- *I succeeded with a very difficult piece of work*
- *I was high up in the mountains*
- *I was on Ayers Rock in Australia*
- *I stood on the podium at the Olympic Games*
- *I was looking at Van Gogh's 'Sunflowers'*
- *The sex with my partner was fantastic*
- *Sun, sea and sand*
- *I was in a church and prayed.*

Life energy in flow

What connects all of these moments? The group found the following answers to this question:

- Only the here-and-now is important
- Time seems to stand still; the past and future lose all meaning
- The experiences are very intense
- Words aren't required to interact with other people
- The people are filled with love and gratitude
- The world isn't so important
- Fear, shame, pain, disgust, anger and rage all disappear
- We didn't suffer.

The final point is especially important in the context of Logosynthesis. Why do we suffer? Is there a state, a mode of being, in which we have to suffer less? Is it possible to suffer less? I gave these questions a lot of consideration during Logosynthesis' development. As I now understand it, *we suffer physically and mentally if we lose awareness of our Essence.*

Our body

We're a physical body with the needs of the material world – food, drink, relationships, the avoidance of danger and the desire for reproduction. Our body is entirely directed at the functions of biological *survival* as both individuals and a species. Biology and medicine examine this body with empirical methods: as matter, as a machine, or as a complex system, an interaction between matter and energy. Science's methods don't fundamentally differ between humans, animals and plants.

Our mind

We're a mind as well as a body. We process and combine sensory inputs from the outside world and can adapt to these inputs; we can sense and cope with rain and drought, with warmth and cold. We can actively alter our environment and shape it almost at will. We're able to formulate personal and collective goals and make every effort to achieve these goals in time and space.

We can approach the mind with rational means. Scientific psychology is concerned with individuals, while sociology and anthropology explore people in their natural and cultural environments.

Our Essence

We're even more still. Since the beginning of human history, an Essence, a higher Self, a true Self, an immortal soul, a divine spark has been at the foundation of human experience. We are beings outside of time and space who continue to develop without end. We can actively shape our world with creative intention. Our world takes on the shape that we need for our Essence's everlasting learning. Life has a meaning and makes sense, and this knowledge lies within us, often hidden. It can only be examined inwardly and imparted by the individual. Science has no place when it comes to examining this perspective: scanning a meditating person's temporal lobe will give as little information about that person's experience as the magnetic properties of my computer's hard drive will give about the book that I'm currently writing on that very same drive. We approach our Essence via other means. There aren't just the classical avenues such as meditation, mysticism and contemplation. Loving relationships, dreams, art, culture, work, dance and sport are also paths to the Self, our living Essence. If these paths are blocked to you, if your past dulls your awareness of Essence, Logosynthesis can open new doors.

The task

Essence, the Source, the living Self, is what differentiates a living body from a dead body – a user from a computer. Essence turns the naked ape into a person. It gives him a task, a calling that provides his life with purpose and meaning. We humans start out in contact with this all-encompassing nature as our original Self. We still know what we really are: *immortal, invulnerable and omnipotent.*

This innermost being is neither male nor female. It knows no age. Such awareness is not sustainable for long in the Earth Life System. We land on Earth with a bump. The body is unknown to us when we first come into being; we don't understand the world around us and we don't possess any form of language. We can't stay aware of our Essence in this situation. The signs that everything is different in this world are simply too strong:

- We receive our mother's physical and mental world in an unfiltered manner for our entire time in the womb. This isn't a problem if everything's going well for her. But if she's depressed or she poisons the fluid around us with nicotine from her cigarettes, things go badly for us as well – and we don't know why.
- During the last phase of pregnancy, the womb keeps us in an extremely tight space without a perceptible exit.
- Our way through the birth canal is very narrow and extremely painful for a long while. If we get stuck, this experience is associated with desperation.
- After birth, the body is sensitive to hunger and thirst but has little freedom of movement.
- The mind – particularly at the start – only has a limited capacity for understanding people and its environment.
- We're dependent on our parents for our physical and mental needs. Desires for food, warmth, cleanliness and care will rarely be fully met.

The awareness of our Essence provides no direction for dealing with this distressing and unfamiliar world. It seems not to apply for this body and mind. The experience of birth and our postnatal needs are so overwhelming that awareness of our Essence and its wisdom rapidly declines. It sometimes seems as if we're nothing more than body and mind – as if we no longer exist as Essence.

Our Self will normally retain awareness of Essence in some form, along with a hint of our task in this world. The American consciousness researcher Charles T. Tart covered these points when writing about our learning in and around the body:

We are living this embodied life for a purpose, a purpose that has something to do with learning – learning knowledge and more importantly learning how to love. Disembodied states of consciousness are wonderful in some ways but awfully vague in other ways, making it harder to learn some things. A physical body provides focus, a stable platform for learning, so that the mind – the Essence, the soul, whatever we call it – is modified by the learning and growth this body facilitates.

A flow of energy

Our timeless Essence manifests itself in this world as our Self. The Self has a body and a mind with which to shape life in three dimensions.

A permanent connection exists between our Essence and our Self – a flow of energy, information or awareness with Essence as the inexhaustible Source.

Our connection to this life energy appears in many forms, as images, symbols, bodily experiences, emotions, fantasies, memories or actions. According to Eric Berne, the founder of transactional analysis, life energy can exist in any manifestation as *free, bound* or *potential* energy. Translated into Logosynthesis, you can understand Berne's terms as follows:

- Your *free energy* is available for the fulfilment of your life task. You know what you're living for if your contact with the world is based on free energy. Your life task unfolds before you and you effortlessly make choices from the wide spectrum of possibilities offered by everyday life that take you further along your life path. In the state of free-flowing energy you draw on abundant resources, and an experience of all-encompassing love and deep gratitude sets in. Your Self, your lived Essence, guides your body and your mind.

- *Bound energy* is the opposite of free energy. Bound energy stabilises you. It creates both your identity and stable patterns within your perception, your emotions, your thoughts and your actions. You know who you are and what's expected of you. Stability is calming, but this calm is deceptive as soon as you stop developing. Bound energy can hinder or delay the fulfilment of your mission within this existence – especially when the energy is bound up in painful memories, frightening fantasies, blocking beliefs or frozen physical or emotional patterns.

Potential energy doesn't flow but can be turned into free energy. You'll become aware of your potential energy when you've discarded old burdens but haven't yet focused on a new goal.

The flow of energy determines life and death. A living cell and a dead cell are almost identical in their chemistry, but if your life energy stops flowing, you die.

In a living cell, millions of chemical reactions serve your growth and development. A dead cell simply disintegrates into its atomic and molecular components: 'ashes to ashes, dust to dust'.

Imprints and their formation

Energy flow is determined by development in early childhood. A baby needs to find language for the plethora of images, sounds and sensations that bombard his or her senses.

A supportive social environment will help the newborn to understand and label this unfamiliar world. The child saves and processes sensory inputs from people, objects and events as helpful representations: *imprints*. These imprints arrange our perception and allow us to think, feel and act in a constructive manner. The following exercise will give you an idea of what's meant by such constructive representations or imprints.

EXERCISE: AN IMPRINT OF A LOVED ONE

> Think about the people who are currently in your life and select someone you love from this group. Examine what happens when you imagine this person and then answer the following questions:
>
> - *Where do you perceive the person in space? More within you, in front of you or behind you? More to the left or the right? Move above you or below you?*
> - *How far away do you perceive the person?*
> - *How do you know that the person is there? Do you see, hear, sense, touch or even smell or taste the person?*

You now have an example of an imprint. Many different answers are given when I present this exercise to training groups. Most people 'see' their loved one, but there are also people who 'hear' their voice or claim to sense their energy like a flow of air or a shock wave. Sometimes the representation of the loved one is found in someone's own body – in their stomach, in their heart – but it's mostly found in the space around a person.

Every person, object and incident in our lives can lead to the formation of an energy structure in space. The combination of all of these structures gives us a map for our path in life. This map can be distorted, full of blank areas and unnecessary detours – or it can provide exact and detailed representations of the outside world.

Reactions to imprints

We perceive energy constructs of people, animals and objects. They're invisible, silent and untouchable to our bodily senses. We notice them with what's commonly referred to as our 'mind's eye'. Imprints trigger physical, emotional and cognitive reactions. We know that they're there – consciously or unconsciously – and they move us. The following exercise will help you to discover your reaction to the imprint of your loved one from the previous exercise.

EXERCISE: YOUR REACTION TO THE IMPRINT OF A LOVED ONE

Return to the representation of your loved one from the last exercise: the image, the voice, the sensations. This time examine how you *react* to the representation of this person:

- *What happens in your body when you perceive this representation? Tension? Relaxation? Vibration? Warmth? Where in your body?*
- *How's your breathing? Shallow? Deep? Flowing or obstructed?*
- *How's your heartbeat?*
- *What emotions do you perceive? Joy? Excitement? Peace? Warmth? Love? Gratitude?*
- *What thoughts do you have?*

The resources of your body and mind will be fully available to you, which is typical for a new imprint and your reaction to it. Various parts of your brain – the brain stem, the limbic system and the cerebrum – will be in tune. You'll be in contact with your own Essence but also able to recognise the other person's Essence. *Love is seeing others as God intended.*

Wouldn't it be wonderful to have a similar relationship with everyone?

The ideal world for a child

The Indian medic Bhava Prakasuka described the unborn child with words that touch me time and time again:

The unborn child is a divine being. This is why its parents shouldn't see their own lives as central. They should furthermore always steer clear of fear and all forms of excitation, both physical and mental. The parents are there to prepare a suitable dwelling for the divine being from their own bodies and souls. They need to see their personal and family lives as cells of divine atmosphere – full of calm and peace, joy and delight. If they satisfy their responsibility in this way, the child will continue to live in his or her eternal homeland even while on Earth. The child will continue to be full of Satchitananda, of absolute existence, knowledge and beatitude – and his or her consciousness will be at rest in boundlessness, continuing to enjoy the blessing of Heaven in the womb.

What normally occurs in our society is more mundane. Even the best parents are sometimes overwhelmed with balancing the child's needs, their own desires and economic constraints. If they can't encounter the child in his or her higher nature – and this is a human condition – the child will no longer understand the world. This is how suffering arises:

- Lack of food, warmth, security, and care lead to suffering. The small child wants to belong and depends on others to satisfy its needs. The child's awareness of the omnipotence and invulnerability of its Essence declines when needs are left unfulfilled. These powers will then be projected onto the environment instead. The parents will be elevated while the child's own power is reduced to worthlessness and invalidity.

- The child is dependent on ignorant, insecure, ill or loveless caregivers for his or her physical and emotional security. Suffering grows as a result; the caregivers just aren't capable of satisfying the child's needs in the Earth Life System. His or her environment also isn't up to this task.
- The child will initially try to bring about satisfaction of his or her needs. But a child can only cry – and if that doesn't work, cry louder. If the parents fail to respond, it doesn't take long for passivity and resignation to result.

Our awareness of Essence and its task diminishes throughout this process. If we're unable to maintain awareness of the original Self, something needs to happen to prevent us from completely losing the will to live. Humans therefore seek refuge in special mechanisms that allow them to adjust to this earthly existence: introjection and splitting off. This brings us to the next principle of Logosynthesis.

Chapter 4 in brief:

- Humans are beings beyond time and space: Essence, a higher Self.
- You have something to discover, to develop or to learn: a call, a vocation, a task, a mission in this world.
- When you enter this world, you need support to find your way within it.
- If you receive this support, you remain in contact with your Essence and your life energy flows freely. You then form realistic representations of the world for direction: imprints.
- If you lack this support, your life energy is bound, representations are distorted, and suffering arises.
- Logosynthesis frees life energy and works to increase awareness of Essence along with the corresponding realistic representations of the world.

5 How your being can break apart

> Just as we tend to assume that the world is as we see it, we naively suppose that people are as we imagine them to be. In this way everyone creates for himself a series of more or less imaginary relationships based essentially on projection.
>
> -- C.G. JUNG

The second principle of Logosynthesis

Awareness of Essence declines through introjection and splitting off.

I COVERED THE REQUIREMENTS FOR CONSTRUCTIVE DEVELOPMENT OF THE PERSON IN CHAPTER 4. It's rare for all of these requirements to be met. The Original Self must struggle to identify and handle experiences in the physical world, and it needs help from other people to be successful. The second principle of Logosynthesis becomes active if no such help is available.

Introjection and splitting off are dissociative processes. We've known about these mechanisms for more than a century as a result of the work of Pierre Janet, Sigmund Freud and Carl Gustav Jung. Logosynthesis details the mechanisms as follows:

- There are events, objects and persons that people see as threatening, painful or dangerous.

- An affected person's body and mind enters a state of alarm when these events, objects or persons are noticed.
- The limbic system in the brain attempts to process the incoming stimuli in a constructive manner.
- These coping mechanisms are insufficient for removing the stress source or reducing the threat.
- There's no help available for coping, e.g. when parents are absent, aren't up to their tasks or even resort to violence.
- The state of alarm then leads to the splitting off of life energy from the Original Self.
- This split-off energy becomes bound up in two types of structure that hinder the flow of energy and are inseparably bound to one another.
- The first energy structure is the *introject*. This stores frozen representations of sensory input from the outside world in the moment of exasperation: pictures, sounds and memories of touches, smells and tastes.
- The second energy structure is the *split-off part*. This is entangled with the introject and stores *reactions* to frozen representations of the outside world: bodily sensations, emotions and thoughts.
- These energy structures can be reactivated by events in a person's current environment. The current environment will then be associated or connected with energy structures from earlier events and lead to similar reactions – physical, mental and emotional.
- The affected person loses direct contact with his or her current environment.
- They instead react as if the old stress sources were present in the here-and-now.
- Reactivation of the old reactions leads to suffering.

Reactions to painful and incomprehensible events therefore become split off from the Original Self. These reactions are then stored with the memories of the events that caused them: the introjects. Contact with Essence is limited or broken off as a result.

Logosynthesis contributes to the re-establishing of this contact. We neutralise the old representations of the outside world and the reactions that are associated with these representations. Deirdre's story provides an example of this process.

Example: Deirdre's fear of boarding the wrong train

Deirdre once boarded the wrong train and has been afraid of doing the same again ever since. She examines the history of this fear during a session with me. A memory emerges: she'd once been trapped in a lift while she was moving a piano. She couldn't breathe and had started to think, 'I'm lost'. Another, earlier incident occurred during nursery school. Her father had taken her to the school but left without saying goodbye. She'd thought, 'I'm lost' and had begun to feel fear and panic then, as well. This thought of being lost was what lay behind her fear of boarding the wrong train. Logosynthesis helps her to dissolve the *introjects* – the distressing old representations of the lift, the piano and her father. Her fear then abruptly disappears. Deirdre now pays careful attention to where she wants to go before a train leaves. She can relax prior to departure without having to get up and check the train's destination. She also remains calm during the journey. She knows that she's well prepared.

In Deirdre's case, the scenes in the nursery school and the lift contributed to the formation of *dissociative structures*. The subconscious activation of these structures led to her fear about the trains. The Logosynthesis sentences released the frozen ties that existed between old memories of the outside world and challenges in the present. Deirdre can now calmly think back to the old images without reactivating her old panic.

The suppression of painful memories

When painful memories surface, we feel the same pain that we did when a distressing incident first occurred. People around us then don't understand why we act in a certain way and are unable to fulfil our needs. We end up jumping out of the frying pan and into the fire. If this pattern is repeated, we eventually form new parts that completely suppress the painful memories and are better received by the people around us. This *second order dissociation* gives us the advantage of no longer needing to feel the pain of the original memories but still enables us to receive at least some degree of care.

We can suppress all memory of an original pain if we adjust to expectations, work hard, make an effort and complete tasks quickly. We can move through the world and receive respect, affection and perhaps even admiration.

Second order dissociation suppresses painful elements of our consciousness and creates a substitute for the love and affection that was missing when we entered the world. But the connection to Essence unfortunately remains broken, in turn making us dependent on validation and judgment from our environment. How do we manage to suppress painful experiences?

- Working hard
- Striving for success
- Finding seemingly rational explanations for personal problems
- Adjustment to other people's desires
- Perfectionism
- Irrational accusations
- Abuse of alcohol and other substances
- Unexplainable fits of rage
- Formation of limiting beliefs such as *No pain, no gain*.

Second order dissociation patterns remain active until they can no longer suppress painful memories. People can work until they burn out or drink until they're fired, and only then will their underlying pain come to the surface. It's at this point that we can apply Logosynthesis with any chance of success. As long as a pattern continues to be lived actively, awareness of and contact with the suppressed past experiences will remain too weak.

Introjects

People are often unable to understand distressing events and receive no sympathy or support in processing these events. Their sensory perceptions of the events subsequently freeze into *introjects*, rigid energy structures. Life energy is required to form these introjects, and this life energy is split off from Essence's great flow. Fantasies about what could or should have happened are also tied up with the frozen sensory perceptions. When a mother threatens to place her daughter in a children's home, the imaginary sensory perceptions that the child associates with this threat are bound up with his or her living fantasy of wasting away in such a home.

Introjects are created if your existing life experience is insufficient to process events and no one who understands and supports you is available to provide assistance. Introjects can be reactivated in later life and provoke similar reactions. The daughter in the last paragraph may have the image of her threatening mother reactivated thirty years later if her partner makes threats of divorce.

Introjects from childhood

The most important introjects are formed during our early childhood as a result of our interactions with our parents. Our parents are normally close to us and bear responsibility for preparing us for independent roles within society.

To fulfil their responsibility, our parents impart their worldview to us via what they say and how they behave. We form imprints as well as introjects in our interactions with our parents. Sometimes our parents' behaviour is supportive, while on other occasions it lacks sensitivity. We learn to copy their words, attitudes and actions. We do the same with other reference people:

- Parents, grandparents, siblings
- Teachers, police officers, colleagues, bosses
- Doctors, therapists, counsellors
- Entire school classes or individual classmates.

We create images and voices of all of these people in our personal space, gradually crowding this space with talking statues. These representations are frozen structures that are made from our own life energy. When we have to reorient ourselves in life, we compare the new with the familiar and so activate the representations that subconsciously seem relevant to the present.

It's important to note the difference between activated imprints and activated introjects. Activated *imprints* signify respect for ourselves, for others and for our environment. They enable us to act and react in accordance with the requirements of the world around us, both autonomously and creatively. When we activate *introjects*, our energy is bound up and our reactions are pre-programmed. We behave in exactly the same ways as we did in past situations.

Introjects in adults

We form introjects when an event shakes our existing frame of reference. This can occur when our employer dismisses us, our doctor tells us that we're in bad shape, or when a lover unexpectedly wants to end a relationship. Introjects can also emerge in many people at the same time. If you're reading this book, you will have consciously lived through 11 September 2001. If I ask you to think back to that date, you'll know precisely how you found out about the attacks on the Twin Towers in New York City. You'll probably find it easy to recall your reaction to that event. I still remember exactly how my wife rang me at my practice at three o'clock in the afternoon. She said that I needed to come home because something terrible had happened. Five minutes later I was sitting next to her in front of the television, watching as the second Boeing 767 slammed into the World Trade Center's South Tower. It literally took my breath away. We knew that something in the world had changed significantly in that instant, even though we couldn't yet guess at the moment's full importance.

If you're older, you'll remember the death of Princess Diana, the first moon landing or the assassination of John F. Kennedy on 22 November 1963. You'll know where you were when you found out these pieces of news and you'll easily be able to reactivate your reactions. All of these events formed introjects and are attached to physical and emotional responses. These responses will immediately re-enter your consciousness whenever you think back to the events or something similar occurs.

Fragments of perception as introjects

Introjects don't have to represent people, objects or events in their entireties. Parts of our sensory perceptions can freeze: the loud voice of a teacher in primary school, an angry mother's contorted face or a hand hitting a child. Words can also become deeply buried in our experience of the world (e.g. 'Idiot!') as well as sentences that comment on our abilities (e.g. 'You'll never make it'), sentences that award us specific qualities (e.g. 'You're stupid') and sentences that associate our identities with other people (e.g. 'You're just like Aunt Martha'). The last example is reassuring if Aunt Martha is clever, but it becomes a banner under which to gather misery if she's ill, lonely or an alcoholic.

Unwanted transgressions of our personal space create extremely powerful introjects, e.g. with sexual abuse. Such introjects can be reactivated any time, in sexual activity or with our own children.

Introjects aren't limited to humans

It's not just humans that leave traces in our energy systems. All possible sensory experiences and their rational and irrational processing can be stored as energy structures. Such introjects then produce standard emotional responses that can limit our freedom. Examples includes places where people have lived or worked:

- Houses or parts of houses – kitchens, bathrooms, cellars
- Landscapes, trees, roads, fountains
- Buildings – schools, hospitals, prisons.

Introjects can also form if children are abandoned by their parents and are left surrounded by strangers. What they first perceive is their physical environment without their parents, as in Deirdre's case. Institutions and the messages that they promote can equally form introjects:

- Churches, political parties, employers
- Abstract concepts – guilt, sins, marriage, divorce
- Values – freedom, progress, chastity
- Media messages
- Television, newspapers, advertisements, the Internet.

I wanted a few days' seclusion while I was working on a book several years ago. I found a hundred year-old spa in Ticino in Switzerland's sunny south. It was an extremely unlucky choice, as the spa's architecture was so similar to my previous workplace at an alpine hospital in Davos that I was confronted with the past at every turn. I didn't know about Logosynthesis back then, so it required considerable effort to free myself from these intense images and focus instead on my work. The following example from Lydia similarly shows how a spatial reality – a wide road – can become an introject.

Example: Lydia and the wide road

Lydia takes part in a training group but struggles to interact with the other participants. When she examines this difficulty, she remembers living next to a wide road as a child. Crossing this road was very dangerous. The traffic was fast and her parents were afraid that something would happen to their only child. All of her playmates lived on the other side of this road, and the separation made Lydia feel sad and alone. This old sadness is reactivated in the group. She feels excluded from interaction with the other participants and sees herself as being on the other side of the road once more. With the help of Logosynthesis she's able to dissolve the wide road introject and begin to interact with the group.

Foreign energy in introjects

Introjects aren't just created from our own energy. They also contain foreign energy – energy from people, animals and objects in the outside world. Parents literally invest energy in their children and end up leaving this energy in their children's fields.

People are rarely able to differentiate their own energy from that of the people around them. They perceive other people's energy as if it were their own. Logosynthesis allows us to remove this foreign energy. Harriet had a serious fear of mice and told me that she wasn't the only person in her family with this fear. Her mother had also had to run from these tiny creatures throughout her life. Harriet applied Logosynthesis to remove her mother's energy and fear from her own energy system. She experienced immediate relief; her fear of mice had been fed by an introject of her mother.

As a curious sceptic, I had to become accustomed to how people can leave foreign energy in our systems and how we can react to this energy in physical and mental ways. It was certainly a strange idea! But it doesn't even stop there, as it isn't just people that leave traces in our system. It's also surgical instruments that are used to operate on your stomach, a dog's teeth in your leg, a kitchen knife in your index finger or a car's bumper on your knee. You'll find a few incredible examples of this in Chapter 23, which covers the application of Logosynthesis to bodily symptoms.

The media, advertising and the Internet

The media generates imprints and introjects as well. Our direct sensory experiences only cover a very small part of the world, and the media shares the rest with us. Advertising in particular constantly tries to install new introjects with the intention of activating them when we go shopping. We prefer to buy familiar brands over unfamiliar brands. We allow the pretty images on TV advertisements to make us believe that we could be similarly happy if we bought the product that's being shown. If an advertisement introduces new terms such as 'irritable bowel' or 'sensitive skin', we tend to discover these new symptoms in our bodies and then look for further information from other sources such as the Internet.

Frozen worlds

Our bodily sensations, emotions and thoughts also freeze in response to our frozen perceptions of unprocessed and traumatic events. These reactions similarly turn into energy structures.

Such structures take life energy from Essence's great flow. They're firmly bound up with the introjects that have stored the perceptions of the events. A frozen world is created in time in space – a 'time capsule' in which the flow of energy between Essence and our Self is impaired or broken off. The time capsule also impairs the exchange of energy between our Self and our environment. It blurs boundaries. We no longer know who or where we are in the most literal senses of these ideas. A part of us exists in the past and in a different place.

Frozen worlds form a filter for our perceptions of the here-and-now and activate our re-experiencing of the past. If you experienced a major fire in your house, any smell of burning will activate this frozen world and you'll immediately respond as if your house were burning once more. Everyone knows such frozen worlds. The following exercise will help you to deepen your understanding of this topic.

EXERCISE: EXAMINING A FROZEN WORLD

> Concentrate on an event that caused you concern when you were a child of around 7-12 years old. Take a few minutes to answer the following questions and write down your answers. The first questions concern your reactions to the event.
>
> Questions about your body:
>
> - *What effect does this memory have on your body?*
> - *Where on your body do you notice this reaction?*
> - *How does the event affect your breathing?*
>
> Questions about your emotional reactions:
>
> - *Which emotions come up when you remember this event: fear, sadness, guilt, shame, disgust?*

Questions about your thoughts and beliefs:

- *What did you think about yourself and others back then?*
- *How would you have liked to have responded to the outside world?*
- *How would you have liked the outside world to have reacted?*
- *What fantasies dawn on you?*
- *Are you familiar with these reactions?*
- *When have you reacted in a similar manner on other occasions?*

You'll normally have reacted with these feelings, emotions and thoughts for many years. This exercise can be the first step to their dissolution.

The following questions concern the triggers for the reactions that you've discovered above. Which representations of the event trigger emotional and physical reactions within you?

- *What do you see when you think back to the event?*
- *What do you hear in the situation?*
- *What do you feel on your skin? Warmth, cold, pressure, vibration, currents?*
- *What do you smell?*
- *What do you taste?*

The frozen world is the combination of representations of the outside world with your physical, emotional and mental reactions. When you apply Logosynthesis, you'll learn to neutralise or even dissolve such experiences. You'll then free the energy that's bound up in the frozen worlds, releasing it for the satisfaction of your personal life task.

The Self

Our Essence is immortal, invulnerable and omnipotent. It's permanently developing, and our presence on Earth is a sign of this permanence. We call our Essence's first form in Earth's three dimensions the *Original Self*. The Original Self remains intensely connected to our Essence; the life energy flows. When we grow, we repeatedly split off energy from this Original Self and store it in frozen worlds.

The main current of life energy continues to flow and absorb experiences. The result is our adult, living *Real Self*. This Real Self contains what's left of our Original Self after numerous splits. It continuously develops and has access to our real life exposure to constructively processed information, events and experiences. It also has the ability to set boundaries in the here-and-now if there's a threat of danger. The Self is clearly aware of the boundaries and connections that exist between itself and others. It lives in the here-and-now and knows its place and task in the world.

Who's in your driving seat?

Life doesn't make sense without awareness of Essence. If this is missing, we're determined by the needs of our body, by the limitations of our mind and by the demands of our environment.

Many people claim to know exactly how to think positively, live your dreams, resolve conflicts, manage your time, allow your creativity to flow, and bravely take action. Why don't these things work? They're clearly explained in how-to books, and they should be simple to understand if the guru explains his or her ideas well. But why don't you do what the guru says?

Frozen worlds normally form barriers to clarity about ourselves. Old, unconscious and split-off parts don't know who we are or why we're in this world. We fail to take control of the wheel as we drive through everyday life – and we instead allow ourselves to be driven around by obligations to other people. The Real Self doesn't need a recipe to plan its time or realise its mission.

Consciousness research uses the term 'Executive' for the inner controlling authority. You'll already know this term from another context: in a company the CEO is the *Chief Executive Officer*, the head of the executive organ – in contrast to the Board that maps out strategy. Are you able to determine your priorities in accordance with your Essence? Or do you bounce from the external world to an introject, from an introject to a dissociated state, and then from one to the other?

Many people are powerless in everyday life. They lost their power to their parents who determined what they had to feel, think and do. When their parents grew older or died, their introjects took their parents' place as guides. The introjects were transferred to other authorities and they ultimately became unable to distinguish other people in their worlds from the frozen images of their past. Their boss took on the place of their father, while one of their colleagues became their mother. The following exercise will allow you to check whether this situation also applies to you.

EXERCISE: THE PAST IN THE PRESENT

Place two blank sheets of paper on top of one another on a table. Now think of someone with whom you have difficulties – in your family, in your circle of friends or at work. Picture this person on the topmost sheet. The paper will remain blank, but allow the image of the person to take shape in your mind's eye.

Move onto the next step when the image has become more or less clear. Now find out who this person reminds you of in your original family. Try to see this second person on the bottom sheet, through the picture of the first person on the top sheet.

Separate the two images when the second image has become clear. Do this by slowly bringing the sheets away from one another. The image of the person with whom you have difficulties remains on the topmost sheet, while the image of the person from your past moves onto the lower sheet.

Now move the sheets completely apart from one another and allow your eyes to rest on the previously lower sheet that bears the image of the person from your past. Examine your reaction to this image.

Finally move your eyes to the other sheet and examine your reaction to the person in your present-day life. How do you now react to this person?

On completing this exercise, many people report that their reaction to the person from their present-day life has become calmer and less fearful or hostile. They can now separate the real person in the here-and-now from the old and frozen introject. You'll be able to make a decision about how you react to the person in the here-and-now; the executive power will finally lie in your hands. If you can see the external world directly, old reactions will no longer be activated. If this is what you want, Logosynthesis can offer a rapid means of achieving your goal.

Chapter 5 in brief:

- Your body and mind can be overwhelmed by events.
- If there's a lack of support during these events, life energy is split off from Essence's main flow.
- The split-off energy becomes bound up in representations of the events and reactions to these representations.
- The frozen representations of the events are called 'introjects'. The reactions are called 'split-off parts'.
- Introjects and reactions are entangled with one another and together form frozen worlds.
- Introjects can be activated by events that are similar to the original events. This activation triggers the same reactions as were experienced in response to the original events.
- Logosynthesis stops past or imagined events from causing such activation.

6 How energy freezes in space

> A brother asked Abba Rufus: "What is inner peace and what use is it?" The old man replied: "Inner peace is to remain sitting in your cell with fear and knowledge of God, avoiding the remembrance of wrongs suffered and pride of spirit. Such peace is the mother of all virtues."
>
> -- EVAGRIUS, AS QUOTED BY DANIEL HELL

The third principle of Logosynthesis

Split-off parts and introjects are frozen energy structures in space.

SPLIT-OFF PARTS AND INTROJECTS AREN'T ABSTRACT CONCEPTS IN LOGOSYNTHESIS. They're viewed as real, three-dimensional energy structures either within your body or outside of it in your personal space.

You partly create these realities yourself. You split off energy from the great stream of your own Essence and bind it in representations of a reality that was painful, threatening or incomprehensible. Others can help to create these realities as well. Parents may need their children to satisfy their own requirements or have a substantial interest in their children making something of themselves. They end up leaving their mark in their children's energy systems.

If we free our bodies and personal spaces from such frozen structures, the inner peace from the quotation at the start of this chapter comes into our lives. The personal space of the *kellion*, the monk's cell, is filled with memories and fantasies that stand between people and experience of Essence in the here-and-now. The emptiness of the cell is a potential environment in which to examine and dissolve these frozen worlds. The following exercise will increase your understanding of your personal space and allow you to better understand Logosynthesis' third principle.

EXERCISE: YOUR PERSONAL SPACE

> Find a space where you can move freely around an area of at least 12-15 square metres. The space can be inside or outside. Walk around the space slowly a few times and then find a place in its middle with clearance in all directions.
>
> Now examine yourself within the space:
>
> - *What emotions do you feel? Fear, anger, sadness, joy, shame…?*
> - *What do you feel in your body?*
> - *Are you tense or relaxed?*
> - *Where is the tension?*
> - *How is your breathing? Deep or more shallow? Fast or slow?*
>
> Next find the boundaries of your personal space. If someone else were to enter the space, where would it begin? Where do you experience the boundaries of your space?
>
> - *In front of you? Behind you? To your left or right?*
> - *How do you know that there is a boundary there?*

- *What differentiates your personal space from its environment? Does it feel warmer? Colder? Denser? Does it seem lighter or darker, more colourful, more transparent? Does it have a different vibration from the world that surrounds it?*

Now imagine various people within your personal space. Choose an important person from your life, e.g. your mother, father, partner, child, a friend, your boss. Examine how this person appears within your personal space:

- *Where exactly does the representation of this person appear in space? In front of you? Behind you? To your left or right?*
- *How far away from you is the image of this person?*
- *How do you know that this representation is there? Do you see, hear, feel or smell it?*
- *With which body sensations, emotions and thoughts do you react to the image of this person within the space?*

Explore the following questions to examine emotions such as fear, rage, hurt, shame, disgust or joy and bodily sensations such as warmth, cold, pressure or pain:

- *Does your breathing change when you concentrate on the perception of the person in your space? Does it become faster or slower? Deeper or more shallow?*
- *Can you move the image or the voice to a different place? Do the emotions or bodily sensations change?*
- *Imagine that the image or the voice disappears entirely from your personal space. How does your state change?*

Repeat this exercise for another important person. You'll then sharpen your perception of introjects in your energy field and your reactions to them.

Energy blocks in space

If someone experiences a traumatic event, energy from their Essence can split off, move to another location and freeze there. This is what happened with my client in Chapter 1; Leonore was literally *beside her shoes* when she tried to open the shower cubicle on the morning of our consultation.

Split-off parts and introjects are energy forms in space. They're found in the body, they overlap with the space that's occupied by the body, or they're found outside of the body. They can also be found further afield, as will be clear from Eric's situation in the following example.

Example: Eric and the lost finger

Eric was an enthusiastic volleyball player. He'd broken the little finger on his left hand while on the court – a typical volleyball injury. The finger became stiff and immovable once this had happened several times. He had an artificial joint inserted, but he could still only move the finger with considerable pain after many weeks had passed.

When he applied Logosynthesis, it became clear that a part of the finger was located behind him, to the left and at shoulder height as an energy structure. When the ball had collided with his finger in the heat of the game, life energy had split off from the finger and created a separate, frozen structure in space.

I invited Eric to say the Logosynthesis sentences to bring the energy back to where it belonged. He immediately felt warmth in his little finger and his pain reduced. He could move the artificial joint freely just a few days later. Six months down the line, the finger was completely healed.

I was quite astonished when we found the finger's split-off energy as a thought form in three-dimensional space. The third principle of Logosynthesis was subsequently confirmed when we were able to guide this energy back to the right place and heal the finger as a result.

Example: Leonore remembers a rude doctor

This second example from Leonore shows that introjects are also spatial. During one of our sessions, Leonore told me about her fear of an upcoming spinal examination. Two of her vertebrae had been injured in an accident. Her fear was caused by the memory of a doctor who had examined her rudely in the past. When she described her fear of another meeting with this doctor, she moved her head to the right – as if someone to her left was talking at her loudly and she was trying to evade him. When I asked her where she perceived the doctor to be in space, she made a movement towards her left ear and recalled how the doctor had bellowed at her from that direction at a mere distance of some thirty centimetres.

In Leonore's energy system, an energy construct of the doctor was really present in space and her body went on to react to this perceived presence. Her fear of the new examination immediately disappeared when I asked her to remove the representation of the doctor from her personal space. Leonore subsequently underwent the examination without encountering any problems.

The body reacts to introjects

My experience with Leonore taught me that it's not just a person's own parts that can be located elsewhere in space. Representations of important people and aspects of our environment can also be stationed within our bodies and personal space. These energy structures seem real to the people that they affect – as real as if the imagined people were actually there. The body tends to react as if these imagined people were really present as well.

The doctor was present as an energy construct within Leonore's personal space, and his energy ended up having a genuinely negative effect on her well-being. The next step was to remove this man's energy from her space. This is how I discovered the third principle of Logosynthesis:

Split-off parts and introjects are frozen energy structures in space.

There are two aspects to this principle:

1 Our awareness that our Self and its energy are not always in the same places as our physical bodies in three-dimensional space. The Self can fragment into parts. These parts can contain real characteristics of memories from the past, can exist as imaginary constructs, or can show up as symbols or metaphors. Each of these parts or aspects can be processed with Logosynthesis.

2 People and objects are represented as energy constructs in the three-dimensional space that surrounds us. When these representations cross a certain boundary in space, they begin to affect our thoughts and feelings as if they actually existed within that same space. We call *personal space* all of the space that exists within this boundary. Introjects are especially powerful if they bind up significant amounts of energy from ourselves or other people or invade our personal space. This can occur as a result of violence, sexual abuse or surgical procedures.

Example: Irma and her personal space

Irma explained to me during one of our sessions how she'd created an exercise for herself. She'd lay down a rope in a circle and then stand in this circle's centre. She defined the circle as her personal space. When she first started the exercise she ensured that the circle surrounded her very closely. She then experimented with how big she could make it without feeling uncomfortable. She noticeably relaxed once she learnt to expand her personal space during the course of her psychotherapy.

Our boundaries are spatial

Irma's example shows that we perceive a part of the space around ourselves as our own. If people, objects or their representations are found in this space, we react to them in a more direct and intense manner than we would if they were situated at a greater distance.

Introjects can exist in our immediate vicinities within our personal space or even overlap the very space that our bodies occupy. Introjects rarely lead to emotional or out-dated reactions when they exist outside of our personal space.

It would be important for the monk mentioned at this chapter's start to free his personal space within his hermitage from the shadows of his past, his desires and his fantasies. Only then would he be able to encounter a higher power in its full and boundless form.

Cleaning up with Logosynthesis

Logosynthesis dissolves frozen energy traces from the past and clears our boundaries. The sentences can help you to take back your energy from frozen worlds and redirect it to the energy flow of your Self. You'll also be able to remove foreign energy from your body and personal space and retrieve your energy that's bound up in your reactions to these structures – before you take it away to the right place within yourself.

You, your Self, will remain in possession of your creative intention's full power. You'll recognise your actual life task with ease; your Self will take over the responsibility.

Chapter 6 in brief:

- Energy that's split off from the main flow of someone's Essence will form structures in multi-dimensional space.
- This applies to energy that's bound up in representations of a person's perceived and imagined world (introjects) as well as in reactions to these introjects.
- These energy structures can also be created or strengthened by split-off energy from other people or objects.
- Logosynthesis dissolves these frozen structures in space, leaving you with genuine freedom within your personal space.

7 How words work miracles

> Sleeps a song in things abounding,
> ever dreaming to be heard.
> All Earth's music starts resounding,
> if you find the magic word.
>
> -- JOSEF VON EICHENDORFF[1]

The fourth principle of Logosynthesis

Words and sentences have an active, shaping effect beyond their content and emotional meaning.

LOGOSYNTHESIS' EFFECT IS BASED DIRECTLY ON THE CREATIVE POWER OF WORDS – without conscious thinking or any other form of focusing your intentions being necessary.

We're all familiar with language as a means of describing our world, sharing our experiences, formulating concepts and establishing theories.

---

[1] http://www.nytimes.com/2013/12/25/arts/music/the-met-orchestra-performs-mahler-at-carnegie-hall.html

Many people find it inconceivable within our basic model of the world that words should have another significance and effect over and above thought. But this is the major difference between Logosynthesis and many other methods of personal change and development.

If the three previous principles of Logosynthesis were somewhat unusual, the fourth is certain to be the least familiar. Many people demonstrate fierce resistance to recognising and accepting this principle. Our usual way of thinking is simply too strongly embedded in a cognitive understanding of words and their functions.

The non-miraculous worldview

The principle of an independent and creative power of words has been a component of many religious and spiritual traditions for thousands of years. The Enlightenment pushed this principle into the background and reduced people to a biological body and an abstract mind.

René Descartes' famous statement *cogito ergo sum* – I think therefore I am – equated the ability to process information with the existence of the thinker. The human bio-computer's user essentially became its software. This perspective allowed us to investigate patterns in humans and the natural world that hadn't been questioned or searched for during the Middle Ages. The sciences that emerged from the Enlightenment still tend to reduce human nature to researchable patterns. Language became a unidirectional means of transportation within this worldview. The Czech philosopher Vilém Flusser bitingly referred to this development as 'the darkness of reason'.

The third dimension of our existence – Essence, the Higher Self – remained by the wayside in the non-miraculous worldview of the post-Enlightenment world.

Words manifest their speakers' intentions

We can also consider words from a different perspective: we can view them as being able to manifest, to create, *by being spoken*. We don't find this perspective in linguistics, psychology or philosophy.

There are numerous links between words and creation or development in religious and spiritual traditions. Words have a power that transcends all cognitive frames of reference in these traditions; the world comes into being through words. Words then assume an inconceivable potential. The creative intention that's contained within a word's form is the very principle of the creative act. Words are even directly equated with God in the first verse of the Gospel of John:

In the beginning was the Word,
and the Word was with God,
and the Word was God.

Words have the property of focusing and actively manifesting the creative intention, the designing will of their speakers, and without stress or rational effort. God's words exercise a direct effect on the material world and even create this world. Words are similarly the creative principle in other traditional scriptures, for example in the Old Testament, Genesis (1,3):

And God said:
Let there be light, and there was light.

The Qur'an is similarly clear on this point (6,73):

When Allah decides something, He just says:
'Be!' – and it is.

In religious and spiritual traditions, the word in itself enables creation from consciousness – *without any processing of content as we know it.*

The creative power of the word was self-evident for a long time in human history. Etymology, a branch of science that researches the origins and meanings of words, offers further links.

Words and development in etymology

Etymology examines the roots of language. It reveals interesting links between language forms for words and language forms for creation, development and growth. The words for 'word' and 'coming into being' are very similar in many languages; in German the words are *Wort* and *Werden*, while in Dutch they're the even closer *woord* and *worden*. The 'word' has the power to create.

A comparable relationship exists between 'saying' and 'blessing' in German and Dutch. In German the words are *Sagen* and *Segen*, while in Dutch they're *zeggen* and *zegen*. If I give my blessing to someone through what I say, I actively bring about something good as a result.

The Dutch similarly have the same word for 'sentence' and 'sense': *zin*. In Greek, the words *arche* (start) and *logos* (word, speech, sense) share the same roots. Words create sense and meaning. Linguists can continue this list indefinitely.

Words and people

Knowledge of the formative and 'magical' power of words survives stubbornly in spite of its 'proven' unscientific nature:

- People have prayed for thousands of years to have their wishes fulfilled and to achieve their goals. Current research proves this effect without being able to explain it.
- Blessings and curses are attempts to bring other people either good or bad fortunes.
- Many small communities still know of women who have a reputation for being able to 'talk off' warts – uttering words over them to make them disappear.
- Certain cultures in the Middle East know of individual words that lead to the immediate paralysis of scorpions when they're said aloud.
- Hypnosis, suggestion and autogenic training have a direct effect on bodily functions.
- Japanese people believe that words have their own spirits. This phenomenon is called *Kotodama*.
- There's only one real magic word for children across the world: *abracadabra*. But did you know that this saying is actually *avrah ka dabra* in Aramaic, which means: *I create what I speak*?

Words in Logosynthesis

Logosynthesis falls back on this long-known knowledge. It directly uses the creative power of words as an instrument:

- To retrieve your energy that's bound up in old representations which are activated in the present
- To remove foreign energy from your body and personal space
- To retrieve and reintegrate the energy that's bound up in your reactions to old representations.

Logosynthesis' precisely worded sentences change our perceptions, emotions and thinking. They shape reality as they're spoken. This goes over and above common, content-based understanding and makes Logosynthesis unique as a method for personal and spiritual development.

> ### Chapter 7 in brief:
> - The power of words is a universal principle of creation.
> - Words focus, manifest and shape the intentions of their speakers.
> - Logosynthesis uses this principle to dissolve frozen energy structures and focus people's subjective experiences on the here-and-now.

8 How we dissolve structures

We dissolve energy structures, but how do we do this?

It's simple to say that Logosynthesis dissolves distressing energy structures and restores the flow of life energy, but how do we do this? These are the steps:

- We identify suffering – blocks in the flow of life energy that take the form of distressing emotions, physical symptoms, limiting beliefs and associated behaviour patterns.
- We recognise energy structures in space that activate these blocks.
- We dissolve these distressing frozen structures and establish contact with our Essence, making use of the power of words.

We carry out these tasks by using precisely worded sentences with the following purpose:

1 To restore the person's energy that's bound up in the energy structure.

2 To remove energy that comes from other people or objects and is part of the structure.

3 To restore the person's energy that's bound up in all of their reactions to the structure.

This gentle procedure frees your life energy. It changes both the blocking structures themselves and people's physical and mental reactions to them.

You'll subsequently discover the next layers for processing or will arrive in the present as an entire being. When the latter occurs, you can further intensify the effect by using a fourth sentence to adjust all of your systems to your new state.

Steps in the Logosynthesis process

This all sounds fantastic, but also abstract and unlikely. How can merely saying simple sentences aloud have such an effect? I don't know how to answer this question myself, but thousands of experiences – not only my own – confirm this ancient knowledge with almost every application of Logosynthesis. Words really do have the potential to alter people's thoughts and feelings in a lasting manner.

Turn back briefly to Cleo's self-coaching experience as covered in Chapter 3. Such a process is typical in the application of Logosynthesis. It contains the following elements time and again and again:

- The person identifies suffering – an unpleasant emotion, a physical symptom, a distressing memory or a limiting fantasy.
- This suffering disturbs the person on their journey through life – in their personal development, in their job or in their interpersonal relationships.
- The suffering is connected with frozen patterns of thought, feeling or behaviour. Alternatives don't seem to be available.
- Clear, calm thinking about one's own person in the present reality is reduced or entirely absent.
- Intuition is blocked.
- A certain aspect of the suffering is identified during the preparatory phase and focused on as a topic for the Logosynthesis application.
- The suffering is associated with a trigger – a representation of a memory, a fantasy or a belief.
- The person derives the exact formulation of the three Logosynthesis sentences from this representation.
- The person says the sentences aloud, without emphasis and at a normal conversational volume.
- The person enters a type of trance state whenever they say one of the sentences aloud. Observers will often recognise this state from the person's rapid eye movements.

- The trance ends spontaneously after a period of between 30 seconds and several minutes.
- The trance allows the sentence to take effect, and once it's finished the person has an altered perception and assessment of the situation that led to their suffering.
- Physical symptoms are reduced and emotions become less intense.
- There are also displacements: the person can feel rage instead of fear, or shame instead of rage.
- Thinking becomes clearer and is more strongly focused on the present.
- The process sometimes leads to an awareness of other memories or fantasies. These then form the start of a new Logosynthesis cycle.
- There will often be a noticeable reduction in the level of distress that's caused by the symptoms that were treated in the cycle.
- The application is ended with a new assessment of the person's current life situation. Constructive behavioural alternatives will easily or even spontaneously emerge from this new assessment.

The above description contains seven key aspects that also describe the seven requirements of any Logosynthesis application:

1 Clear a space
2 Zoom in on the suffering
3 Examine the triggers
4 Say the sentences
5 Allow the words to take effect
6 Reassess the topic
7 Shape the future.

Part III will teach you how to practically apply Logosynthesis by using these seven requirements.

In the next chapter I describe a session with Tony that provides another example of a Logosynthesis application. You'll be able to recognise all of the above-listed aspects in my account, just like in Cleo's story. Tony's case also shows how Logosynthesis cycles can sometimes bring past triggers of a current topic to the surface.

> **Chapter 8 in brief:**
> - Blocks in the flow of life energy can be dissolved with precisely worded sentences.
> - We can discern seven requirements, phases or aspects within this dissolution process.

9 How Tony suppresses a memory

Tony's presentation

TONY IS A THIRTY YEAR-OLD MANAGER AT AN ENGINEERING COMPANY. He's good at his job and valued by his colleagues and boss. He's worked at the company for seven years and participates in many projects.

In a few days, Tony will present a project of his own to management for the first time. He's worked on the project for many months, and he's convinced that it's great and will bring the company many new orders. He becomes nervous as the Monday of the presentation draws closer. He sleeps badly and dreams of the board members throwing eggs and tomatoes at him. Strangely enough, some of the attackers in his dreams are former classmates from his school days.

Tony wakes up sweating and with a racing heart. He's now had the nightmare on four occasions. He continues to struggle with the presentation back at the office. When Friday evening comes around, he even considers giving up. His colleagues watch him and wonder what's wrong, but they fail to recognise his distress. After they've left, Tony's mind continues to create scenarios that correspond to his worst nightmares. The confident Tony of days gone by now seems nothing more than a distant memory.

He participates in an introductory course to Logosynthesis at the weekend because he wants to learn about self-coaching with this new tool. He considered not attending the course due to the upcoming meeting, but he made the decision to come along nonetheless. I teach the group about the principles of Logosynthesis and Tony volunteers to take part in a demonstration. He's under great pressure, so he asks me for help with his performance. I invite him to sit in a chair in front of the group and explain his story. I then ask him to envision doing the presentation before I present him with a series of questions:

- *What's happening in your body?*
- *What emotions does the vision trigger within you?*
- *What are you thinking?*
- *What's the worst that could happen?*
- *How much are you distressed – on a scale from 0 to 10?*

Tony responds in a sweat. His heart is racing and he feels a knot in his stomach. His body is quite clearly in a state of alarm. He's afraid and ashamed and he thinks that he's a loser. A fantasy emerges when I invite him to explain further: his boss makes fun of his presentation and his colleagues laugh at him and think that he's a loser as well. He now rates his distress as a 9 on the scale from 0 to 10. I ask Tony to explore what he perceives in the space around himself:

What's triggering this severe reaction?

Tony describes perceiving his boss to his right and his colleagues in a semi-circle around him. While he talks, he notices that the knot in his stomach tightens further. I now formulate the first Logosynthesis sentence and ask Tony to repeat it:

I retrieve all my energy bound up in the representation of this imaginary scene with management and take it back to the right place in my Self.

Tony pauses after he's said the sentence. He allows the sentence to take effect and watches what happens. After the pause, the knot in his stomach loosens and he yawns. Yawning is a well-known sign of relaxation. I then give him the second sentence:

I remove all non-me energy related to this imaginary scene with management from all of my cells, from my body and from my personal space, and I send it to where it truly belongs.

Tony breathes deeply once more and watches what happens. After he's paused to let the sentence take effect, he reports that the knot is still there but that he feels less fear. I then give him the third sentence:

I retrieve all my energy bound up in all my reactions to this representation of this imaginary scene with management and take it back to the right place in my Self.

Now something remarkable happens: Tony suddenly sees an image of his former teacher, Mr. Mayer, instead of his boss and the team. He remembers Mr. Mayer as a tyrant. I help him to recall the memory in more specific terms:

- *Where in space is the representation of Mr. Mayer? In front? Behind? To the left? To the right? Above you? Below you?*
- *How far away is the image?*
- *How do you know that he's there? Can you see him? Can you hear him? Can you feel him?*

Tony responds immediately: "He's to my right. He's bigger than me and is teasing me in front of the entire class. He's mean. All of the children are making fun of me, and the teacher's laughing with them!"

The first cycle has uncovered an old memory – a video clip that's tightly entangled with emotions of fear, humiliation and abandonment. I give Tony the first sentence:

I retrieve all my energy bound up in the representation of Mr. Mayer and the children who make fun of me and take it back to the right place in my Self.

Tony closes his eyes for a full two minutes after he's said this sentence. His eyes move rapidly below his closed eyelids. After a while he takes a deep breath, opens his eyes and looks at me. I now give him the second sentence:

I remove all non-me energy related to the representation of Mr. Mayer and the children who make fun of me from all of my cells, from my body and from my personal space, and I send it to where it truly belongs.

Tony takes another long pause and allows the sentence to take effect. His face and shoulders relax. When he reopens his eyes, he looks peaceful and liberated. He tells me that the knot in his stomach has disappeared. His heart's beating more slowly, and although he still thinks that he's a loser, he holds this belief with less intensity. I give him the third sentence without probing any further:

I retrieve all my energy bound up in all my reactions to this representation of Mr. Mayer and the children who make fun of me and take it back to the right place in my Self.

This sentence doesn't need long to take effect once it's been repeated. Tony opens his eyes after just 20 seconds. He now feels calm and confident. I ask him to think back to the situation at school. He shrugs his shoulders and laughingly says: "Mr. Mayer had a problem." I then ask him to concentrate again on the scene of the presentation to management. He does so and shows no trace of fear, a knot in his stomach or any similar sign of stress. He remains confident and composed. Between sips of a large glass of water, he says: "I'm not afraid any more. I was scared of my teacher back then. Now I look forward to presenting my ideas in the meeting. They haven't asked me to do so for nothing, and it's a good chance to show off my skills!"

The problem appears to have been resolved. Tony is now fully in touch with his competence as a professional. His life energy is flowing freely, so it's the right time for Logosynthesis' fourth sentence. I tell him the sentence:

I tune all of my systems to this new awareness.

Tony says the sentence aloud and allows it to take effect. His relaxation continues to an even deeper level. He sighs, and when I ask him if we can stop at this point, he thanks me and returns to his place in the semi-circle with a wide smile on his face.

I receive an email from Tony a few days later. The presentation to management was a total success. Tomatoes and eggs were still involved, though – his boss invited him out for lunch.

The memory is neutralised

This case is typical of how Logosynthesis is applied to a distressing memory. The work goes a step further than the process in Chapter 3, as Cleo only dissolved a fantasy. A disturbing memory from a long left-behind classroom shone through during Tony's preparation for the presentation. He was overwhelmed by this painful event as a child because no one was there to support him at the time. His past experience in the classroom was subsequently reactivated in the present. Tony experienced exactly the same emotions, thoughts and physical reactions in his vision of the management meeting as he did back in the classroom all those years ago.

Logosynthesis' carefully prepared and worded sentences helped Tony to access the earlier situation and neutralise the distressing memory. The previously subconscious image of Mr. Mayer lost its influence over the current situation. Stress responses no longer appeared. After Tony had applied Logosynthesis, the story from the classroom became irrelevant to his current task. He became able to register the reality of the situation in the present and deploy his capabilities to their full. In the next chapter I'll cover what may have taken place in Tony's brain.

Chapter 9 in brief:

- It's clear from Tony's case that the memory of a distressing past experience can lead to problems when it comes to dealing with other people in the present.
- Logosynthesis can help to neutralise past experiences.
- The intervention made all of Tony's potential available for his current task.

10 Understanding the brain

Connections with brain research

I'M OFTEN ASKED HOW LOGOSYNTHESIS CONNECTS WITH THE LATEST DEVELOPMENTS IN BRAIN RESEARCH. There are no simple answers to this question.

Logosynthesis' concepts are based on working hypotheses. The existence of Essence isn't provable with current methods, no one's measured the energy structures that are presented here, and we only know of the power of words from holy books.

I can nevertheless carefully formulate a few assumptions about processes in the brain based on existing research. When we identify and activate a distressing topic, a much more complicated version of the following takes place within our brains:

- Information about the present reality is collected by our senses. It travels through the thalamus to a small organ in one of the oldest parts of our brain: the amygdala.
- The amygdala compares information from the incoming sensory stimuli with stored experiences from the past. This process allows it to identify threats to our survival.
- In a present reality that's perceived as threatening (in this case Tony's presentation), the person activates a subconscious memory (being bullied at school). This memory is now reactivated and re-experienced – all subconsciously!
- The amygdala triggers an alarm as a result of the perceived threat. This alarm prepares us to fight, flee or freeze.

- Connections to the brain's higher centres are impaired in this state of alarm. The hormone cortisol disrupts the connection to the hippocampus, which is the next station for processing information.
- The hippocampus is responsible for organising the flow of information under normal circumstances. This organisation isn't possible during a state of alarm in the amygdala. In our example, Tony can no longer think.
- The person therefore reacts to the present challenge with simplified, reflex patterns:
  - Fight, flight, freezing or splitting off.

I presume that the following occurs during the application of Logosynthesis:

- The information in the amygdala's archive that's responsible for triggering the alarm is neutralised or erased. The amygdala is then unable to trigger the same alarm in the future.
- Incoming information that concerns a new challenge is forwarded to the brain's higher centres without impairment. Tony can assess his situation in an adult way.
- The brain is in a state of equilibrium once more and the person can meet the challenge in the here-and-now with his or her full potential. Tony presents his ideas to management with composure, competence and confidence.

Chapter 10 in brief:

- Our brain learns and records which situations are dangerous during our development.
- An alarm is triggered if an event is assessed as being dangerous.
- The perceived threat will sometimes not correspond to the present reality. This error leads to an inappropriate reaction.
- Applying Logosynthesis reconciles the perceived threat with the present reality.

PART III

LEARNING LOGOSYNTHESIS

Seven requirements for success

I OUTLINED SEVEN REQUIREMENTS FOR CONSTRUCTIVE WORK WITH LOGOSYNTHESIS IN CHAPTER 8. These requirements form the basis for how Logosynthesis is applied in self-coaching. Long-term alleviation of symptoms requires all of the following:

1 *Clearing a space* provides a vessel for Essence's healing effect – where everything that is can simply be.

2 *Zooming in on the suffering* helps you to find specific issues in your life on which to apply Logosynthesis.

3 *Examining the triggers* identifies perceptions towards which you react with suffering. It also determines the content of the first three sentences.

4 *Saying the sentences* initiates the processing and reorientation stages.

5 Once the sentences have been spoken aloud, the pause for *allowing the sentences to take effect* prompts an autonomous, subconscious reorganisation of physical, emotional and cognitive structures. You consciously observe this reorganisation with curiosity and patience.

6 *Reassessing the topic* helps you to evaluate the application's effect. It also activates new perspectives that help you to find the next topic.

7 *Shaping the future* is about considering how to implement Logosynthesis' results on an everyday basis. Reflection is the key to remoulding previously blocked aspects of your life.

You'll become closely acquainted with these seven aspects of Logosynthesis over the course of Part III. This section provides you with a step-by-step guide to carrying out your first full Logosynthesis cycle. When you've completed the section you'll be able to practise with your own topics – and before long you'll be applying Logosynthesis every day and to all kinds of problems.

11 Clear a space

Curiosity and patience

EVERY LOGOSYNTHESIS APPLICATION BEGINS WITH A CLEAR SPACE. You release yourself from your everyday concerns for a moment. You set aside time in your calendar, you find a quiet place and you prepare a jug of water. You then open yourself up to what emerges within yourself, reassured by how:

Everything that is may be.

Are you afraid of something? Okay. Are you annoyed? Even better. Are you sad? That's alright. It's just something that's happening. The starting point for all applications of Logosynthesis is characterised by two words: curiosity and patience. You don't do anything, you don't direct anything, you don't guide anything, you don't judge anything and you don't condemn anything. You don't even try to achieve anything. This is paradoxical to a culture in which many people believe that happiness has to be actively created.

Essence takes control

If you clear a space for the work within yourself, you allow your true Self, your Essence, to take the lead over your life. It then becomes easier to reach a state of happiness:

- You know exactly what you want – and what you don't want.
- You recognise opportunities to advance on your path and you make use of these.
- You're in good and open contact with the people around you and you minimise interpersonal conflicts.
- You can isolate yourself if necessary.

- You can support others if this is more important than fulfilling your own needs.
- You can get help when you need it.

Logosynthesis works from the basic stance that your Self knows what's important.

The power of old emotions

If you lose awareness of Essence, fear, sadness, anger, guilt and shame take control over your behaviour in society. This isn't apparent at first glance. Fear can hide itself in the following manners:

- You have your life under control
- You prefer familiar solutions – regardless of whether these are the best solutions
- You tend to avoid pain and unpleasant states of mind
- You're impatient.

Many people try to cover up painful emotions: anger, greed, addiction and the yearning for power and control are all used for this purpose. They don't offer a long-term solution. Logosynthesis can help you to let your Self become active, permanently and consciously.

This process doesn't just help with the solving of problems, but also with your personal and spiritual development. Access to your Essence always opens up new dimensions and qualities of human existence regardless of what's happening in your life. The process will never stop for as long as we live; it's our stairway up to Heaven.

Learning is practising

Practise Logosynthesis at every opportunity. Collect small successes. When you're working on topics from your own life, do so in small steps.

Your trust in the method will then grow, and with time you'll be able to apply Logosynthesis to bigger issues. If you attempt to do too much at once, the effect will fall flat and your motivation will fail. A simple tip:

Take smaller steps if the application of Logosynthesis leads to impatience, anger, irritation or sadness.

The patterns that are disturbing your life and which you want to change are often patterns that you've practised for your entire life. They freeze a significant amount of your life energy. When you start to apply Logosynthesis, you often only have access to a small amount of your Essence's limitless energy. You'll need more of this energy to tackle your bigger topics. The more of your Essence's energy that flows, the easier your work with Logosynthesis will be.

Your application of Logosynthesis will be more effective and efficient – especially at the start – if you follow a few simple rules:

- You take your time
- You create a clear space
- You start with small topics
- You apply it to everything that disturbs you
- You pay attention to small changes
- You stick with it!

Practice makes perfect, and this notion applies to Logosynthesis as well. Start by consciously working with small topics. This will help you to become familiar with the method and give you practice with its processes. When the whole process becomes automated as a result of your repetitions, you can then begin to concentrate on bigger issues from your life.

As you continue to practise, applying Logosynthesis to small topics will begin to only take a few minutes. Bigger topics will require more time. Some sources of suffering are so large that they can keep people captive for their entire lives. I see such topics as collections of numerous smaller topics that you can dissolve in succession. Work with this question in your mind:

How do you eat salami?

The answer? Slice by slice – and slices that are overly thick are difficult to digest. If you don't like salami, use:

How do you eat artichokes?

Leaf by leaf. Then you reach the heart, the finest part.

If you practise with small topics for a good while, you'll eventually come to notice that familiar distressing emotions diminish. One of Logosynthesis' major advantages is that you can collect small achievements right from the start. These successes will confirm that you're on the right path.

The iceberg phenomenon

When people start to apply Logosynthesis on themselves, they don't usually expect quite so much unfinished business to be lying below the surface of their everyday lives. New topics appear after every application. This is normal and the result of how our subconscious mind works. The subconscious has a good method for preventing unpleasant experiences from disturbing us at every opportunity: it suppresses them. It costs a lot of energy to keep the lid shut on these experiences, but they have to stay sealed away until we have another means of dealing with them.

Your subconscious mind learns that unfinished business can be processed as soon as Logosynthesis becomes active in your life. Like with a melting iceberg, new material constantly makes its way to the surface. The subconscious keeps pushing up frozen worlds to advance its own development. The emergence of old memories and emotions is therefore a sign that your subconscious mind has recognised Logosynthesis' potential!

You're not the suffering

It's sometimes difficult to recognise your results because the melting iceberg is driving so much unfinished material to the surface. A return to the principles of Logosynthesis then becomes important. Remember that frozen, distressing patterns in feelings and thoughts are unnecessary energetic structures – and that you can dissolve them step by step.

After the melting of the iceberg with its dissolution of old and frozen worlds, a new world appears *by itself*. This new world offers many more opportunities because all of your knowledge, all of your life experience and all of your Essence's potential are now available. Your life energy flows freely. You can perceive precisely and think clearly. You can assess other people correctly and your actions are target-oriented. The first principle of Logosynthesis therefore becomes profound knowledge:

Our true being doesn't suffer. We suffer because our awareness of Essence is lost.

You're not the suffering. You are Essence. As you continue to practise Logosynthesis, your identification with your old, familiar emotions will shrink. You're not a sad, fearful or quick-tempered person. You may have been in the past, but you only adopted these patterns because you didn't know how to respond differently in a difficult situation.

As you dissolve the patterns step by step, you develop more openness, more serenity and more curiosity. The process uncovers enormous potential – in your relationships, in your work and in your personal development.

I've spent many hours dissolving old patterns and frozen worlds, especially in the first years after I discovered Logosynthesis. My process became faster and faster with time, and it became clear to me that old pains no longer needed to exist.

Possible topics for your self-coaching

Below are several examples of topics for a first Logosynthesis application. I've consciously ensured that they're all about current people or situations. Before you concern yourself with deeper or older topics, it's worth practising how to apply Logosynthesis on real events from the present such as:

- A friend has borrowed something without your permission and returned it damaged.
- An acquaintance is always late while you make the effort to be on time.
- Your daughter's teacher has told you that her schoolwork isn't good enough and you feel responsible for this.
- A friend has promised to perform some music at your birthday party but has then missed the date to travel abroad.
- A colleague has changed the objectives of an important project without discussing this with you.
- Your mother told you point-blank during her last visit that she doesn't approve of your choice of partner.
- Your neighbour has shown you her new car while you'll still have to drive your own pile of scrap for a good few years.
- A colleague has arrogantly dismissed your suggestion for an improvement to operational processes – as if you don't have a clue what you're saying.
- You read in the newspaper about an especially terrible terrorist attack.

EXERCISE: CLEARING YOUR SPACE

Now it's your turn. Take half an hour, disconnect the telephone and retreat to a quiet place. Take a piece of paper, a tablet or a laptop computer and sit down comfortably. Now open yourself up to work on a current topic. Go back in time in your thoughts. Examine a memory from the past few days or weeks and take note of the people and events that provoke disturbances:

- Troublesome emotions: fear, anger, shame, sadness, contempt, disgust
- Unpleasant bodily sensations: a lump in your throat, a knot in your stomach, tension in your shoulders, pressure in your head
- Changes in your breathing: less free, more shallow, constricted
- Distressing, repetitive thoughts.

These disturbances can be about people or events that have caused you a problem on a single occasion or about situations that occur on a regular basis.

Now ask yourself:

- *Am I familiar with this feeling?*
- *Have I experienced something similar in the past?*
- *Does this often happen to me?*

You've found a topic for your first Logosynthesis application if you answer 'Yes' to these questions. Make a few notes about the memories that came up during the exercise and choose one topic to work on.

When you're making your choice, bear in mind that the topic should trigger physical or emotional distress but shouldn't weigh too heavy. You're only practising the method for now!

You'll find it easier to learn how to apply Logosynthesis if you're not overwhelmed by the intensity of the topic that you've selected. The application will become almost automatic as you continue to practise. Only then should you approach more difficult topics. When you learnt to drive, you didn't spend your first few hours doing high speeds on the motorway.

I'll show you how to work on bigger topics later on in this book. Sometimes you'll also need the assistance of a trained specialist.

Chapter 11 in brief:

- The self-application of Logosynthesis requires sufficient time and a quiet environment.
- Your basic stance is one of patient, curious openness.
- You can work with all feelings and thoughts that occupy you, new or old.
- Prepare by narrowing down the topic of the current application.
- It's best to start with a small topic until you've automated the process.
- New topics will continue to appear throughout the application – the iceberg principle.
- Work on big topics with numerous small steps – the salami principle.

12 Zoom in on the suffering

The suffering

YOU CAN APPLY LOGOSYNTHESIS IN ALMOST ALL SITUATIONS AND TO ALL FORMS OF SUFFERING. People suffer both physically and emotionally. Physically there's pain, cramps, pressure and tension, and emotionally there's fear, concern, grief, shame, guilt, rage, disgust and abandonment – all in various degrees of intensity.

People who suffer tend to blank the outside world. They're only aware of their own suffering and their thoughts and behaviours are limited as a result. Only very few people are able to contemplate their own suffering in a calm and rational manner. The perception of someone who's suffering usually contains an element of exaggeration that first strikes in hindsight. Back pains are hellish and fear of flying can make travelling a nightmare – but these horrors are barely noticeable to the people around those affected. Cat owners may experience the grief of losing their pet as almost overwhelming, while other people may just shrug their shoulders at this loss. For sufferers, facts offer little consolation.

We work in accordance with the salami principle when we apply Logosynthesis. We try to split the suffering into small portions that we can then reduce in a step-by-step manner until they're finally dissolved. This approach has two important benefits:

- You always know what you're applying Logosynthesis to
- You can detect every minor development once the application is over.

Many frozen patterns in our thoughts, feelings and behaviours have existed for our entire lives. They can be triggered by a variety of events, e.g.:

- Your partner has a bad day and gives you the cold shoulder. You become unsettled or irritated. You react in the same way if someone fails to respond to an important email. Both events lead to the same reaction.
- You always respond with anger if someone doesn't immediately grasp what you mean. You do this with your partner and also at work.

People often neutralise single situations with Logosynthesis but continue to react with familiar patterns. They then tend to believe that 'nothing's changed' and become disillusioned. The single neutralised situations generally have their roots in earlier events, and it's the people's reactions to these earlier events that can still be triggered.

My own long experience has convinced me that something changes with every Logosynthesis cycle. If nothing seems to have changed, I normally assume that my preparation wasn't sufficiently precise. If this is the case, the affected person can't accurately compare the world before and after Logosynthesis has been applied. It's difficult to recognise changes if you don't closely examine the current suffering and its triggers. The iceberg looks just as it did before even if it's actually shrunk by a metre.

Meta-questions

I've developed two *meta-questions* to help my clients more precisely describe both the suffering that they experience and its triggers. We'll address the first meta-question in this chapter.

A meta-question covers a group of questions that you can use to zoom in on and more closely describe a topic or situation. It's easier to notice changes if you compare your answers to the meta-questions both before and after you apply the Logosynthesis sentences.

I recommend that you answer the questions in detail. You'll become acquainted with your own patterns as you repeat the process and you'll then know which questions are most important for you.

Meta-question A: how are you suffering?

The first meta-question, 'meta-question A', concerns the symptoms of the suffering. It helps you to explore the symptoms and determine their intensity. Your answers will reveal how you react in the given situation and also how you can alter your reactions by saying the sentences. We need this clarification so that we can precisely track any changes that occur. Meta-question A is as follows:

HOW are you suffering?

Meta-question A explores all manifestations of the current suffering – physical, emotional and mental. You'll also assess how distressed you are by these symptoms on a scale from 0 to 10. The following questions clarify meta-question A in further detail:

Questions about bodily sensations:

- *What happens in your body if you concentrate on this person or event? Pain? Tension? Sweating? Shaking? Itching? Where in your body?*
- *How's your breathing? More at the top of your chest? More in your stomach? Are there blocks in your airflow?*

Questions about emotions:

- *What emotions does it trigger within you? Grief? Fear? Anger? Shame? Guilt? Disgust? Envy? Jealousy? Helplessness?*
- *Which emotions are most intense?*
- *With which physical reactions and thoughts are these emotions associated?*

Questions about thoughts, beliefs:

- *Which thoughts, beliefs, fantasies, hypotheses, interpretations and convictions accompany and reinforce the suffering? Are they about you? Are they about others? Are they about society? Are they about anything and everything?*

An assessment of the distress caused by these symptoms:

- *How great is the distress caused by the sum of these reactions on a scale from 0 to 10, where 0 is 'Not distressing' and 10 is 'Extremely distressing'?*

Now it's your turn. Your first self-coaching with Logosynthesis begins with your answers to meta-question A.

EXERCISE: META-QUESTION A FOR ONE OF YOUR OWN TOPICS

In this exercise you'll apply meta-question A to one of your own topics. Concentrate on the event or person from Chapter 11. Your memory of this event or person caused you distress. Your answers to meta-question A will clarify your physical, emotional and mental reactions to this memory. Answer the questions from the previous paragraph and write down your answers for later comparison.

Once you've answered these questions – ideally in writing – you can bid farewell to the distressing reaction for now. Logosynthesis doesn't require you to activate any suffering for longer than the time that you need to answer meta-question A. Then the process can continue with meta-question B and the sentences.

You may have noticed that I've avoided expressions such as 'your suffering', 'your symptoms' and 'your distress'. This is intentional: the suffering isn't yours and you don't need to take possession of it or retain it. You are Essence and your true Self doesn't suffer. This point is covered in further detail in Chapter 4.

Chapter 12 in brief:

- You can zoom in and focus on a topic for self-coaching with the help of two meta-questions.
- Meta-question A is: how are you suffering?
- This meta-question explores your physical, emotional and mental reactions to people or situations.
- You'll end up with an assessment of the suffering on a scale of distress that ranges from 0 to 10.

13 Examine the triggers

> I started to see the heads in the emptiness,
> in the space that surrounded them.
> When I noticed for the first time how a head froze and
> suddenly became motionless, I began to tremble with fear.
>
> -- GIOVANNI GIACOMETTI

THE SCULPTOR GIOVANNI GIACOMETTI SAW HIS SCULPTURES IN EMPTY SPACE BEFORE THEY REALLY EXISTED. He was able to consider them in detail once he'd overcome his initial alarm. All that then remained was to cast them in bronze.

Meta-question B: what triggers the suffering?

You've already answered meta-question A. You've explored the suffering, feelings and thoughts that arise within you in response to a current situation. In the next phase we'll turn away from the suffering and focus on its triggers. This leads to meta-question B:

WHAT triggers the suffering?

Using meta-question B limits the time that you need to deal directly with the symptoms. You don't try to change the suffering; it'll disappear by itself if it's no longer triggered. Let's take another quick glance at the theory:

- Suffering emerges when our contact with Essence is broken off
- Access to Essence is blocked if we react to frozen representations of past or imagined events.

You've explored your reactions and determined that they're associated with suffering. This suffering has physical, emotional and mental aspects and you've given it a number on a scale of distress that ranges from 0 to 10.

The topic isn't the trigger

Logosynthesis helps you to dissolve automatic connections that exist between events in the world and your inner state. Let's take three of the examples from Chapter 11:

- A friend has borrowed something without your permission and returned it damaged
- A friend has promised to perform some music at your birthday party but has then missed the date to travel abroad
- Your mother told you point-blank during her last visit that she doesn't approve of your choice of partner.

How would you tend to react to these events? With grief, fear, shame, guilt, embarrassment or anger? Is one of these emotions more familiar to you than the others? If so, for how long have you known this pattern? How great is the distress on a scale from 0 to 10?

Your answers to meta-question A provide information about this reaction pattern. We now need to explore exactly how this reaction arises. At first it seems strange that it's not the person or situation itself that leads to the physical and emotional reaction. It's actually the frozen perceptions of the people, objects or situations that trigger these reactions – the videos, the representations in your personal space. The following exercise illustrates this fact in a striking manner. It's part of our standard repertoire for seminars on Logosynthesis.

EXERCISE: SOMEONE YOU STRUGGLE TO GET ALONG WITH

> Think of someone who's not physically present and with whom you struggle to get along. This person doesn't take you seriously and reacts incomprehensibly or aggressively towards you. You can't find the correct response to this behaviour and so you react with unpleasant feelings. You can further explore this reaction with meta-question A right now – or you can continue to read on first.

The search for triggers

What's really interesting about this exercise isn't your physical or emotional reaction, as you already know that too well. The interesting point is that the person doesn't need to be present to trigger the reaction. A representation of a person can cause you to react with unpleasant physical symptoms, emotions or thoughts.

We now come to meta-question B, which examines the suffering's *trigger*. In Logosynthesis, we assume that this trigger is an introject, an energy construct in space. Meta-question B helps you to locate this trigger and explore its characteristics. The process works best if you examine the sensory experiences via which you notice the trigger:

- Visual: the sense of sight
- Auditory: the sense of hearing
- Kinaesthetic/Haptic/Tactile: the sense of touch
- Olfactory: the sense of smell
- Gustatory: the sense of taste.

These five modalities of perception ('VAKOG') help you to accurately examine what you're responding to when you suffer. They offer the answer to meta-question B: what triggers the suffering?

Meta-question B is made up of a catalogue of questions just like meta-question A. This time the questions aren't about bodily signals, emotions or thoughts, but rather about energy constructs that contain people, animals, objects and events that trigger physical, emotional or mental reactions. Meta-question B helps you to explore your personal space. Its questions are as follows:

- *If something or someone were to trigger this reaction, who or what would it be?*
- *Where in space? More in front of me? More behind me? More to my left or right? Above me? Below me? How far away?*
- *How do I know that I perceive it there? Can I see it? Feel it? Hear it? Smell it? Taste it?*

Answers to meta-question B for the above-listed examples might be:

The event:

- A friend has borrowed something without your permission and returned it damaged.

The representation:

- *I see the friend in front of me. He's wearing his usual baggy pants and his smell of sweat stings my nose.*

The event:

- A friend has promised to perform some music at your birthday party but has then missed the date to travel abroad.

The representation:

- *I feel my mobile phone in my hand and stare at the text message she sent to tell me that she couldn't come.*

The event:

→ Your mother told you point-blank during her last visit that she doesn't approve of your choice of partner.

The representation:

→ *I hear my mother's sharp voice to my left and see her facial expression.*

In the following exercise we'll apply meta-question B to the topic that you uncovered in Chapter 11.

EXERCISE: META-QUESTION B FOR ONE OF YOUR OWN TOPICS

Think back to your own topic. You've examined and noted down your reactions with the help of meta-question A. You'll now explore the triggers for these reactions and answer the following questions for your perception of the person or situation. You're already familiar with these questions:

→ *If something or someone were to trigger this reaction, who or what would it be?*

→ *Where would it be in space? More in front of me? More behind me? More to my left or right? Above me? Below me? How far away would it be?*

→ *How would I know that I perceive it there? Could I see it? Feel it? Hear it? Smell it? Taste it?*

You'll receive confirmation of the link that exists between your frozen perceptions and your current symptoms if you ask the following questions:

→ *What happens within my body if I concentrate on these representations in space?*

→ *What emotions do I perceive?*

→ *What thoughts come up?*

> If you've stayed on track, your answers to these questions will match with your original reactions in meta-question A.

The process of going through the meta-questions often leads to clarification by itself. Many counselling models make use of this dynamic.

From the meta-questions to the sentences

The meta-questions prepare the way for using the Logosynthesis sentences:

- The answers to meta-question A define your starting position and the associated distress. They help you to precisely determine the sentences' *effects*.
- Meta-question B outlines the symptoms' triggers. The answers help you to determine the *content* of the Logosynthesis sentences.

The frozen memories or fantasies that are uncovered by meta-question B create a goal for the sentences, just like the image of Cleo's boss or Tony's teacher. The next step is to condense your answers to this meta-question into one term or short sentence. For Cleo and Tony these were 'Mark's face', 'Mr. Mayer's voice' and 'the classmates' laughter'. In the previous examples, they could be:

- Michael in his baggy pants (visual)
- The image of the text message (visual)
- My mother's voice (auditory).

Now find a similarly short label for your topic's trigger, and then continue to the next chapter where you'll learn more about the power of words.

Chapter 13 in brief:

- All physical and mental suffering has triggers.
- These triggers are representations of frozen sensory perceptions within your body or personal space (see Chapter 6).
- These representations portray memories and fantasies.
- These triggers lead directly to suffering.
- This suffering disappears if these triggers are neutralised or cease to exist.
- These triggers are examined with the help of meta-question B: what triggers the suffering?
- You can see, hear, feel, smell and taste the triggers.
- Your answers contain representations of how your senses perceive the triggers.
- A summary of your answers to meta-question B determines the content of the Logosynthesis sentences.

14 Say the sentences

Words' creative effect

LOGOSYNTHESIS' TRUE MIRACLE LIES IN ITS SENTENCES AND THEIR EFFECT. The steps listed so far exist in some form within many counselling and self-coaching models. We clear a space in Eugene Gendlin's focusing, we clarify our emotions and bodily symptoms in cognitive behavioural therapy, and the exploration of perceptual structures is best known from neuro-linguistic programming (NLP).

Counselling mostly addresses the content of words. Clients learn to understand themselves and their environments in a new way; their existing frames of reference are rearranged and expanded with the aid of language from a specialist. The power of words in Logosynthesis is based on a far less common principle of action in which words themselves have a power to shape and create. This power is hardly understandable in rational terms, but its effect is unmistakable.

The effect of words continues to fascinate me even after years of working with Logosynthesis. You say a sentence at a normal conversational volume and without particular emphasis – and immediately something changes.

The examples of Cleo and Tony show how Logosynthesis' results develop both during and after the sentences have been said. Both people identified some discomfort, found its trigger and said the sentences. Each sentence was followed by a period in which the sentences took effect. Neither Cleo nor Tony did anything else and yet their memories and fantasies lost their painful charge.

The procedure for saying the sentences aloud

When you're first learning Logosynthesis, say the sentences calmly, at a normal volume and without any emphasis. When you're familiar with the sentences you can also whisper them or even just think them.

After you've said the sentences, close your eyes and allow them to take effect. This pause usually lasts between 30 seconds and 10 minutes and will be different on every occasion. You'll find more information about this pause in the next chapter. Continue with the next sentence when you notice a shift – either your eyes opening or the process feeling complete.

Sentence 1

The first sentence is as follows:

I retrieve all my energy bound up in… and take it back to the right place in my Self.

Sentence 1 retrieves all of your life energy from frozen representations of fantasies or memories. The topic of the first sentence is always the trigger from meta-question B, e.g.:

I retrieve all my energy bound up in this image of Michael in his baggy pants and take it back to the right place in my Self.

or:

I retrieve all my energy bound up in this image of the text message on my mobile phone and take it back to the right place in my Self.

or:

I retrieve all my energy bound up in my mother's voice at the family celebration and take it back to the right place in my Self.

Pause once you've said a sentence. Allow the words to unfold their full power. Relax and watch how the sentence takes effect. Don't do anything, don't try to improve or change anything – just let the sentences work until your eyes open or you feel a change in your body, emotions or thoughts.

Sentence 2

Say the second sentence once the first sentence has taken effect. It goes as follows:

I remove all non-me energy related to… from all of my cells, from my body and from my personal space, and I send it to where it truly belongs.

It's not just your own energy that's bound up in representations of memories, fantasies, and beliefs. Other people and objects also leave behind their energy in your body or personal space. Simply saying Sentence 2 moves this energy out of your system to a place where it truly belongs.

The trigger from meta-question B is once again the topic for the sentence, e.g.:

I remove all non-me energy related to the image of Michael in his baggy pants from all of my cells, from my body and from my personal space, and I send it to where it truly belongs.

or:

I remove all non-me energy related to the image of the text message on my mobile phone from all of my cells, from my body and from my personal space, and I send it to where it truly belongs.

or:

I remove all non-me energy related to my mother's voice at the family celebration from all of my cells, from my body and from my personal space, and I send it to where it truly belongs.

Close your eyes once again and relax. Now observe the sentence taking effect until your eyes open or you feel a change.

Sentence 3

Sentence 3 follows once Sentence 2 has taken effect:

I retrieve all my energy bound up in all my reactions to… and take it back to the right place in my Self.

You explored your reactions to the triggered representation in meta-question A. Sentence 3 retrieves the energy that you've bound up in these reactions and takes it to your Self, e.g.:

I retrieve all my energy bound up in all my reactions to Michael in his baggy pants and take it back to the right place in my Self.

or:

I retrieve all my energy bound up in all my reactions to the text message on my mobile phone and take it back to the right place in my Self.

or:

I retrieve all my energy bound up in all my reactions to my mother's voice at the family celebration and take it back to the right place in my Self.

Now close your eyes again and watch what happens. Observe the process patiently until a few minutes have passed or you feel a change in your body or emotions.

Sentence 4

The fourth sentence is the icing on the cake of self-coaching with Logosynthesis. Only say it when the distress you've experienced has reached 0 on the scale and you feel powerful, alive and relaxed.

You might only reach this state after multiple cycles or once you've processed multiple topics. Sentence 4 is as follows:

I tune all of my systems to this new awareness.

If you say Sentence 4 at the correct moment, it'll normally bring about a further deepening of your new state.

EXERCISE: APPLYING THE SENTENCES

You've already answered meta-questions A and B for your topic from Chapter 11. You can now form and say the Logosynthesis sentences for your topic.

I recommend that you read the next chapter before you do so. It covers the period in which the sentences take effect. You'll then be better prepared for what the sentences do.

The sentences at a glance:

1 *I retrieve all my energy bound up in (memory, fantasy, person, object or aspect) and take it back to the right place in my Self.*

2 *I remove all non-me energy related to (memory, fantasy, person, object or aspect) from all of my cells, from my body and from my personal space, and I send it to where it truly belongs.*

3 *I retrieve all my energy bound up in all my reactions to (memory, fantasy, person, object or aspect) and take it back to the right place in my Self.*

Only say the fourth sentence when the first three sentences have led you into a state of deep relaxation:

4 *I tune all of my systems to this new awareness.*

Chapter 14 in brief:

– Logosynthesis activates healing and development processes through the power of words.

– This effect results from saying three sentences that relate to your perception of a specific person, situation or expectation.

– Saying the three sentences moves your life energy to the correct places within or outside yourself.

– A fourth sentence generalises the effect of the topic's processing across your mind, body and soul.

– The pauses between the sentences are vital for the sentences' effect (see Chapter 15).

15 Allow the words to take effect

> **Everything that was is gone.**
> **Everything that is may be.**
> **Everything that comes may come.**

The pauses are critical

LOGOSYNTHESIS' FULL EFFECT UNFOLDS IN THE PAUSES AFTER THE SENTENCES. These pauses are special experiences, particularly when you first begin to apply Logosynthesis.

Many counselling methods attempt to alter an experience's content by using a conscious alteration of language. You convert passive word choices into active word choices, e.g. 'It always happens to me…' becomes 'I do (something)' and 'I can't' becomes 'I don't want to.' This form of conscious linguistic restructuring is entirely absent from Logosynthesis. Most people can't imagine Logosynthesis' effect because the other manner of using language in guided change is so widespread. When you apply Logosynthesis, your experience changes *by itself* during the post-sentence pauses.

It's important to leave the process up to the power of the words during these pauses. You can observe the process from a certain distance in the same way as you watch clouds move through the sky. You can see shapes, colours or movements – but everything drifts past you.

The most important point about the pauses

You've answered two meta-questions. You now say your first sentence and then you... do nothing. You simply allow the sentence to take effect. You then say the second sentence and allow it to take effect. The same applies with the third sentence. A Logosynthesis cycle therefore contains three sentences and three such pauses. These pauses are vital for allowing the words to work. You don't have to do anything and you also shouldn't do anything during them. You don't need to know where the energy goes; your Self will know. You don't need to add anything, you don't need to construe anything and you don't need to interpret anything. Just relax and settle back. Your cerebrum is on standby. You'll be like the airline passenger from an old song by the Swiss band Taxi:

I take another Campari soda
The sea of clouds lies far below me
The fan hums quietly in the background
It's as if I'd completely ceased to be.

What can happen in the pauses

Participants report experiencing many different effects during the pauses:

- They think about where the 'right place' mentioned in the first and third sentences might be
- New images or memories emerge
- Symptoms are alleviated
- Bodily sensations move from one place to the other
- Images from people in the present fade to images of people from the past
- The original issue appears in a new light.

Allow time for the pauses, especially when you first start out. Simply notice what is – just like how a gardener waters his flowers and allows them to grow, a visitor to a concert enjoys the music, or you surrender to a soothing massage.

Take a break. Your conscious mind can relax and leave the processing to your true Self, safe in the knowledge that the next stage of your development is already taking place. Be open and curious about what a sentence will bring about during this time. Watch with interest what happens within you – in your body, in your breathing, in your heart's rhythm, in your emotions and thoughts.

Also explore what happens outside of your body in your personal space – how images and voices of people, symbols and situations change.

The sentences' effects on the body

Our memories are stored within us, even reaching right down into our cells. An important part of Logosynthesis' effect therefore takes place within the body. Signs that you're processing include:

- Yawning and breathing in deeply
- Stretching
- Vibrating arms or legs
- Relaxation in the neck or shoulders
- A rippling feeling below the top of your skull
- A feeling of a heavy load having been lifted from your shoulders
- A warm flow of energy through your entire body
- A clicking sound in your ears
- A feeling of something distressing leaving your body
- Smiling and other involuntary changes in your facial expression
- An all-encompassing silence; a deep calm.

You'll often experience relaxation as the words do their work and the energy structures dissolve. At least one of the three sentences will usually have such an effect. The first sentence will sometimes increase the tension, but the distress will generally subside after the three sentences have been completed.

When you feel an increase in tension, this means that the sentence that you've just said has uncovered an underlying energy structure – either a memory or a desire. This is normally a positive development even though it doesn't feel like one. Examples of tension increases include:

- Tension or cramps of which you were previously unaware
- Trembling, crying
- A dull and diffuse feeling in your head or body
- Nausea, dizziness, a headache, tiredness, exhaustion
- A knot in your stomach.

These symptoms sometimes point to a new topic, although they're often signs that you simply haven't drunk enough water.

Water as a support tool for the processing

You make demands of your energy system when you apply Logosynthesis. Your system has to rearrange itself because your own energy is returning and foreign energy is being removed. Fresh, clear water helps this process.

Lack of water is often responsible for making you feel tired, dizzy or nauseous during the processing pauses. It's best to drink a glass or two of uncooled, non-carbonated water if this happens. Drinking water increases the conductivity of the neural pathways that run between the brain and the sensory organs.

The sentences' effects on the emotions

The sentences have a similar effect on the emotions as they have on the body. People feel relieved, calm, relaxed, good-natured and happy. The distress reduces and some people can scarcely believe just how much they suffered only a few moments ago.

A distressing emotion will sometimes transform into another emotion that can be equally distressing, e.g.:

- Fear becomes anger or rage
- Anger becomes shame or guilt
- Rage becomes grief or loneliness.

These changes occur during the pauses after the sentences and they mirror the course of normal growth and development. When you overcome fears, you'll often discover that you've allowed others to cross your boundaries. You'll then be faced with the anger that's needed to defend these boundaries. If you're furious because your partner has left you, underneath this rage lies grief and loneliness.

In Logosynthesis applications, such processes often run as if they were set to fast-forward. When you re-assess your situation after you've said the three sentences and allowed them to take effect, be sure to pay attention to which distress now has priority.

New distress will often arise from topics that first surface during the Logosynthesis cycle. The original suffering dissolves, but the new suffering can be just as distressing as its predecessor. You've made a step in the right direction even if it doesn't feel like one. Keep at it!

The sentences' effects on thoughts and beliefs

My clients often demonstrate astounding changes in their thinking. Logosynthesis enables them to think in a more clear, rational and gentle manner. After they've said a few sentences or completed a cycle of three sentences, they often make comments such as:

- *My mother didn't get a lot of affection during her own childhood. I'm not surprised that there wasn't much affection available for me.*
- *My boss is sandwiched from above and below in the hierarchy as well.*

- *The major airlines' planes are checked to an almost obsessive degree nowadays.*
- *I have enough money. This wasn't always the case, but I don't really need to worry that it's not enough any more.*

It's also possible for entire memories to shift and for you to become aware of previously unknown aspects of yourself. This occurred in the following example from Frank.

Example: Frank gets attacked

Frank is a successful sales manager. During his first session with me he talks about a trip that he took through South America many years ago. A criminal gang had enticed him into a dark bar in Caracas with the promise of free drinks. When he entered the bar, he was held and robbed by five women. Only a combination of luck and dexterity had allowed him to make a dive for freedom. As he broke away, the gang member who had enticed him into the bar was talking to two policemen out on the street. The same thing happened to his friend a few minutes later after he went into the bar to look for Frank.

Being robbed – and by women – while the policemen had a relaxed discussion with one of the gang members was too much for Frank. The robbery has had a serious impact on his life and he's even been diagnosed with post-traumatic stress disorder. The disorder manifests itself as panic attacks, especially when he enters an unfamiliar bar. His memories of the bar in Venezuela are then reactivated and he experiences intense physical and emotional reactions. He has to beat a hasty retreat from anywhere that initiates this response.

Frank would simply avoid bars in future if this were his only problem. But he's also no longer able to approach people in a relaxed manner in his job, which is a significant handicap for a manager working in customer relations.

The real reason for Frank's present panic emerges during our session. He discovers an unconscious fantasy that he'd had in the bar in Venezuela: 'They're going to kill me!' A video clip plays before his mind's eye that shows him being bumped off with baseball bats. This fantasy is subconsciously reactivated whenever he enters an unfamiliar bar or meets new people. Frank responds with fear, rage and panic even in friendly environments.

The video in his mind changes after he applies Logosynthesis. Frank now remembers how he celebrated the incident's ultimate good outcome with his friend, out on a terrace under the Caracas sun.

Resistance

Many people encounter resistance in their self-application of Logosynthesis, especially during the pauses between sentences when they can't, shouldn't or mustn't do anything. How the sentences work and that they actually work at all seems impossible in their prevailing, rational model of the world. The power of words can't be explained through biology or psychology. Representatives of these fields rely on terms such as 'suggestion' and 'placebo' to explain its results, and usually without defining what's meant by these terms or attempting to explain their effects. Participants at my lectures and seminars often react sceptically to the first few demonstrations. They just don't believe what they see and hear, even if the people involved – such as Tony – radiantly recount how much better they feel.

It's best to approach Logosynthesis with an attitude of openness and to apply the model on yourself. Do you notice an inner dialogue once you've said the sentences? E.g.:

- *It just can't work!*
- *The other people here have a screw loose!*
- *It's all based on the placebo effect!*
- *You must be a psychologist to invent something this insane!*

If you do, you're obstructing the power of Logosynthesis' words. Are you prepared to give the method a chance even in spite of these sober and seemingly rational arguments? If you are, here are three tips for distracting and occupying your conscious thoughts while the sentences work:

- You can repeat the sentences
- You can count backwards aloud, e.g. from 39 to 17. If this is too simple, count backwards in multiples of 7 from 1000 to 6. The development process can then continue while the sceptic in the left-hand side of your brain is kept busy.
- You can hum a tune, e.g. *You are my sunshine, my only sunshine*.

The right-hand side of your brain takes control when you hum. It has less difficulty with irrational processes than the left-hand side.

Repeating the sentences

There are many reasons for repeating a sentence and its pause:

- You haven't yet found the correct formulation of words
- You've only had limited experience with Logosynthesis
- Your concentration levels reduce and your thoughts wander
- Emotions or inner monologues remove you from your attitude of openness – see above
- A topic is complex or associated with numerous people and situations
- It seems as if saying the sentence hasn't changed anything
- You're uncertain about whether the sentence works.

Some people keep repeating the sentences until they notice an effect, even though saying each sentence one time is enough. This isn't necessary, but it gives the conscious mind something to do.

How long do you pause for the sentences to take effect?

The answer to this question is very individual. The pauses will generally require between 30 seconds and 5 to 10 minutes. I've also seen some pauses need half an hour or longer.

Pauses can be brought to an end in various ways. People report processes of change that occur in their bodies, emotions and thoughts. If no new topics or layers emerge for processing, a pause will come to an end when you feel considerable relaxation and a profound sense of calm.

The O-ring and the traffic light

What do you do if you're not sure whether a pause is over? The O-ring and the traffic light are easy ways of finding out. A muscle test – also referred to as the O-ring – makes it simple to follow the process. Once you've said one of the sentences, hold your thumb and middle finger lightly together on one or both of your hands. Close them with enough pressure to hold a cigarette paper. Then use the power of words to say:

The pause will end when I open my fingers.

As in all cases when words take charge, you don't need to do anything else. Just hold your fingers lightly together and watch what happens. You'll sometimes feel a twitch or an increasing of pressure until the fingers spontaneously come apart. You'll initially doubt whether this happens consciously or subconsciously, but such considerations will become redundant with continued practice.

If the O-ring doesn't work for you, you may like to imagine a traffic light and watch for the colour that it shows before your mind's eye. Processing is still going on for as long as it's on red or amber. You can also discover your own test methods: you might be alerted to the end of a pause whenever you hear a clicking in your ears or feel a flinching on the bridge of your nose.

I always do the O-ring test with both hands. I often find that the fingers on my left hand open before the fingers on my right hand. Why is this? I don't know, but it works. With practice, you should be able to follow the progress of the sentences through each pause.

EXERCISE: AN OPENING SENTENCE

> The following sentence lets you open up a channel for the healing energy of words and the true Self. This way you include your Essence in the solutions to your problems. Use this sentence before every Logosynthesis application. Breathe in and out deeply four times and then say:
>
> *I activate my true Self for my development during this process.*
>
> Now calmly wait for it to take effect, avoiding any special emphasis or conscious intention. Be sure to note all sensory perceptions, physical experiences, beginnings of inner dialogue and emotions that come up during this pause.

Chapter 15 in brief:

- The pauses after each sentence are the most important times in all Logosynthesis applications.
- You don't *do* anything, but you observe a lot.
- The effects are individual and varied – in your body, emotions and thoughts.
- Resistance can block the sentences' effects.
- You can keep such resistance in check by counting or humming.
- It sometimes makes sense to repeat individual sentences.
- The O-ring and traffic light tests help you to define precisely how long the pauses last.

16 Reassess the topic

A reassessment

YOUR FIRST LOGOSYNTHESIS CYCLE IS BEHIND YOU. IT'S NOW TIME FOR A REASSESSMENT. You don't need to analyse anything while you say the three sentences and allow them to take effect – not even if the effects are dramatic. You only return to your initial topic after the third sentence's pause.

The next step is to compare your inner state and its triggers with your answers to meta-questions A and B. You then reassess the level of distress that you experience on the scale from 0 to 10.

Meta-question A: how are you suffering?

Examine your inner state just like you did at the start of the Logosynthesis cycle:

Questions about your physical reactions:

- *What happens in your body if you concentrate on this person or event? Pain? Tension? Sweating? Shaking? Itching? Where in your body?*

Questions about your emotional reactions:

- *What emotions does it trigger within you? Grief? Fear? Anger? Shame? Guilt? Disgust? Envy? Jealousy? Helplessness?*

Questions about your mental reactions:

- *Which thoughts, fantasies, hypotheses, interpretations and convictions accompany and reinforce the suffering? Are they about you? Are they about others? Are they about society? Are they about anything and everything?*

Questions about the distress that's caused by these reactions:

- *How great is the distress caused by the sum of these reactions on a scale from 0 to 10 where 0 is 'Not distressing' and 10 is 'Extremely distressing'?*

How do your answers differ from the answers that you gave before you said the sentences? Are these differences more in your mental, emotional or physical reactions? Sometimes the differences will be striking, like for Frank in Chapter 16. Sometimes the differences will be small, or your overall level of distress might remain on a similar level. If this occurs, take a closer look and ask yourself:

What's the difference in my perception of the triggers and reactions between this 7 on the distress scale and the previous number?

In my experience, numbers that are the same before and after the sentences will actually relate to different aspects, emotions or representations of reality. Frank's distress remained the same after three rounds, but his 8 related to different aspects of the event:

- The memory of the faces of the women who attacked and restrained him
- The fantasy that he'd be killed with baseball bats
- The indignation that one of his attackers was operating in league with the police.

You may get the impression that nothing has changed if you don't prepare the sentences in sufficient detail. I often fail to notice changes when I haven't looked closely enough. Something always changes when Logosynthesis is applied.

Meta-question B: what triggers the suffering?

It's often easier to identify changes in your answers to meta-question B. This is because these answers are so much more precise:

- *If something or someone were to trigger this reaction, who or what would it be?*
- *Where in space would it be? More in front of me? More behind me? More to my left or right? Above me? Below me?*
- *How far away would it be?*
- *How would I know that I perceive it there? Would I see it? Feel it? Hear it? Smell it? Taste it?*

The representations of people or objects will often shift in space – changing their colour or becoming smaller or larger, more transparent or more solid. Voices can become quieter and sounds can disappear. Images, voices and forms can also become clearer. A situation or person will suddenly emerge from out of a grey haze. Tony's case from Chapter 9 is typical; processing a current situation uncovers a memory of an earlier experience.

A new cycle

If you're not content with the result after the current cycle, answer meta-questions A and B again and then proceed with the next round.

You'll often need multiple cycles to reduce the distress of a certain topic to a bearable level. Every distressing situation has many aspects to be neutralised. You'll see this in the upcoming chapters. It's worthwhile processing all of these aspects one after another.

Example: Christian and the car crash

Christian's car had careered into a pileup. He suffered from whiplash that made him unable to work. He was able to neutralise the following aspects of the crash during his work with me, one after another:

- The flashing hazard lights of the car in front
- The image of the car behind him in his rear-view mirror
- The screeching of the brakes
- The noise of car behind's impact
- His body's forward movement
- His body's rearward movement
- The explosion of the airbags when he hit the car in front
- The fantasy that he was going to die
- The injured people in the car behind him
- The police sirens.

The intrusive images of the accident disappeared, his pains became milder, and he was finally able to return to work on a part-time basis.

Will the symptoms return?

I'm often asked this question, but I can only answer with 'Yes and no'. Aspects that you've processed will never be reactivated *in their previous forms*. But if a topic is made up of many aspects, it may seem as if 'the problem' does return.

If you get this impression, cut the salami that is the problem into slices and apply Logosynthesis to multiple aspects. Doing so will help you to reduce the distress that these individual aspects cause.

This is a step-by-step process that may require multiple cycles. The pressure will luckily often be much reduced after your first Logosynthesis application.

Professional help makes sense

You'll inevitably activate hidden frozen worlds when you apply Logosynthesis. Intense emotions and physical symptoms will then emerge. Not everyone is able to recognise these frozen worlds for what they truly are: blocked energy. The worlds appear real and feel real as well. Please be sure to seek assistance if this happens to you.

It's also worth seeking support from a specialist when you're dealing with significant distress. The professional will help you to identify the relevant topics in your answers to the meta-questions and then to form and say the sentences. You'll find a list of trained Logosynthesis professionals on the official website, www.logosynthesis.net. Many of these professionals also work through Skype.

Sentence 4

If you don't need any assistance and are satisfied with your results after a series of applications, it's then time to apply Sentence 4.

You only say this sentence once the problem that you've worked on has been completely dissolved and you've achieved a new level of awareness and relaxation. Sentence 4 brings an end to your Logosynthesis sequence with the following words:

I tune all of my systems to this new awareness.

Now take a moment to relax and observe. Allow yourself to be surprised!

Chapter 16 in brief:

- You reassess the topic after you've completed a cycle of the three sentences.
- You answer meta-questions A and B once more.
- You repeat the procedure with your new answers to the meta-questions if necessary.
- Seek assistance from a trained professional if the distress remains significant over the longer term.
- It's time to say Sentence 4 once the distress has reduced to a 0 or 1. This sentence is the icing on the cake.

17 Shape the future

The vision of the future

FUTURE PACING IS A TECHNIQUE THAT'S BORROWED FROM NLP. It lets you to travel into the future to determine whether your Logosynthesis application has achieved sufficient results. To use the tool, simply imagine leaving the room that you're in and going forwards in time. Now consider a situation that previously caused you significant distress. Is the distress gone? Do familiar reactions reappear? Do new aspects show up?

If you remain calm when you consider the situation, you're likely to stay calm if you actually find yourself in a similar situation again. Alternatively, if you find that the symptoms have only disappeared in part, you know that some of the relevant triggering aspects probably still need to be neutralised. It's then time to return to the meta-questions, form new sentences and allow these sentences to take effect.

Allow yourself to be surprised!

Logosynthesis is based on principles that many readers will find unfamiliar and perhaps even unbelievable. The principles are far distant from the conventional, mechanical, materialistic worldview. But if you're prepared to engage with a different perspective, you'll be rewarded with previously unknown possibilities for change and development.

Let yourself be carried on the flow of Logosynthesis' ideas and exercises. A healthy degree of scepticism is appropriate, as it's only with such scepticism that you'll be able to integrate what you read into your everyday life. Development doesn't occur through the adoption of new ideas, but rather through interaction between the familiar and the unknown. Your prior life experience will help you to absorb and digest new concepts.

Practice makes perfect

With time, many people find that applying Logosynthesis becomes a part of their everyday routines. They also find that their tolerance for destructive patterns is significantly reduced as a result.

The best way of dealing with initial impatience is to apply Logosynthesis systematically to a long list of small topics. You'll then learn when and how it works for you, and your ability to notice small changes will significantly increase. This ability is essential, especially if you want to work with topics that have accompanied you for your entire life.

As time goes by, you'll find that every Logosynthesis cycle has its own effect and that this effect varies. Everything is possible: an escalation, a rollercoaster of emotions, a minor relaxation of the muscles in your neck, or a huge, huge relief that seizes your whole body and all of your emotions.

Just like all good things in life, you shouldn't overdo Logosynthesis. Limit its application to a maximum of 40-50 minutes per day and watch closely for what changes in your daily routine; every change needs time to integrate.

The 51% rule

You become aware of your Essence when you feel that everything makes sense. Your life has a meaning and a goal. You're able to perceive your body, yourself, other people and the world for what they are. They're imperfect, but this imperfection belongs to being on this planet.

You'll make a quantum leap if you come into contact with your Essence for 51% of the time. You'll then be able to see that you're not the part that suffers. You can identify the parts that are stuck in the past or in frozen perceptions. Applying Logosynthesis will really make sense and be enjoyable.

I sometimes compare this position with the investigatory methods used by Peter Falk in his role as TV's Lieutenant Columbo: 'You're afraid of other people? Interesting! I have another question…'

Logosynthesis in practice

Logosynthesis' effect isn't limited to the resolution of individual everyday problems. In my experience, almost every topic has other, deeper topics hidden behind it. Logosynthesis is also an excellent instrument for cleaning up your energy system. As an example, I might say the following sentences after an intense day at work with many different people:

1 *I retrieve all my energy bound up in all representations of all people today and take it back to the right place in my Self.*

2 *I remove all non-me energy related to all representations of all people today from all of my cells, from my body and from my personal space, and I send it to where it truly belongs.*

3 *I retrieve all my energy bound up in all my reactions to all representations of all people today and take it back to the right place in my Self.*

When all of the energy has flowed back to the right place, I say:

4 I tune all of my systems to this new awareness.

Logosynthesis has become a daily activity for me, much like meditation, fitness, yoga or golf for other people. I call it 'vacuuming the soul'. This isn't just something that I do: Buddhist monks have reported that regularly applying Logosynthesis has sped up their meditation process.

In the next section I'll present a range of possibilities for how Logosynthesis can be applied to concrete topics such as fear, rage, relationships, dreams and physical symptoms.

Chapter 17 in brief:

- Practise, practise, practise.

PART IV
APPLYING LOGOSYNTHESIS

Dealing with difficulties

You now know how and why Logosynthesis works and you have your first practice sessions behind you. In this section you'll find ways to apply Logosynthesis to certain problem areas.

No fundamental differences exist when it comes to handling various forms of suffering, symptoms and states. Emotional, physical, cognitive and relationship problems all follow from your interrupted contact with your Essence in the here-and-now. Logosynthesis dissolves frozen energy constructs and restores the flow of life energy as a result.

Nevertheless, specific applications have become clear over time for various areas. It's a little like golf: the swing of the club is in principle always the same, but you have to adapt your play to the terrain. Distressing emotions require a different focus from limiting beliefs, physical discomforts and relationship misunderstandings.

You'll begin this section by working on distressing emotions. Emotions give our lives colour, and many people like to allow their feelings to guide their actions. Such people even fail to differentiate between what they are and what they feel. Herein lies the problem: many emotions bear no relation to a person's current environment but are instead reactions to a frozen past.

In pure biological terms, emotions relate to events in our environment that require an immediate reaction. Fear indicates danger, rage shows that an enemy has crossed our boundaries, shame confronts us with a gap in our understanding of societal rules, and guilt lets us know that we've made a mistake.

The ideas presented here about applying Logosynthesis on yourself aren't set in stone. Consider them as approaches and inspiration for your personal development.

18 Dissolving fear

> **Hopefully it won't get as bad as it already is.**
>
> -- KARL VALENTIN

What is fear?

FEAR IS APPREHENSION TOWARDS SUFFERING THAT MIGHT BE CAUSED BY A PRESENT OR ANTICIPATED THREAT. In biological terms, fear is a mobilisation of the body to cope with real physical threats such as hunger, thirst or dangers from our environment – or social threats such as abandonment or separation from our communities.

We talk about 'fears' when these risks are physically understandable. It can be reasonable to fear illness, accidents, violence, death, war, terrorism or losing someone who's close to us or something that we own. Fear can also be based in fantasy, and so not physically understandable and/or unfounded.

Phobias

We talk about 'phobias' when an irrational fear takes on a serious form. Examples include fears of department stores, lifts, mice, spiders and other people. These fears are often no longer based on genuine risks from our environment, but rather on energy structures that we've stored in our bodies and personal spaces dozens of years ago. This will be clear in the following example from Luzia.

Example: Luzia's fear of falling rocks

During a Sunday outing, my wife, Luzia, and I were driving to a small historical settlement. We needed to travel down a narrow mountain road along the way that had a sheer drop to one side. At the start of the road there was a sign that warned about the danger of falling rocks. Luzia appeared nervous as we drove. When I asked her what was wrong, she replied that when she'd last driven this way a boulder had come off the side of the mountain and landed on the road in front of her. She'd needed to make an emergency stop and then move the rock with her passenger's help. She was now afraid that the same thing could happen again.

This everyday occurrence bears all of the essential hallmarks of fear as a biological warning system:

- Something happened
- The incident presented a danger
- Luzia survived the incident in one piece
- She now expects something similar to occur in the future.

It doesn't matter whether any damage was actually done or anyone was actually injured – or whether these things only occurred in Luzia's imagination. Our brains don't differentiate between historical realities and fantasies when they analyse potentially dangerous situations. Both memories activate the danger warning systems in our brains' limbic systems.

This activation is useful in the case of real risks. A child who receives a burn will learn to fear fire. But we end up suffering unnecessarily when our brains give out disproportionate alarm signals.

Fear and the brain

Irrational fears are alarm responses to irrelevant stimuli. To be 'afraid of certain things' belittles the experience. The fears feel very real: your entire biological being is targeted at overcoming a perceived danger. The limbic system within your brain is on high alert, stress hormone levels are high, and you switch between reaction patterns for fight, flight and resignation. This exact process has protected us from dangers since the start of evolution.

But some things have changed since our time in the savannah. We were previously exposed to dangers such as hunger, thirst, cold and wild animals. We now tend to be overfed and need to protect wild animals from ourselves rather than the other way around.

Fear without danger

When we have a troubling experience – especially as children – our brains tend to trigger alarm responses without the presence of serious danger in future situations. Tony's situation is an example of this tendency.

Your brain's original response makes sense if someone sinister jumps out and demands money at knifepoint while you're walking along a dark street. You'll make an automatic and instant decision between fight, flight and surrender. But this reaction pattern is also present when Tony prepares his presentation for management. It's as if a caustic boss were comparable with a hungry lion.

Logosynthesis and fear

Fear is an important application area for Logosynthesis. So long as there's no real, life-threatening or dangerous situation, we can calmly assume that our fear is a frozen reaction to an energy structure in space. Our true Self knows no fear; it's indestructible and is at peace with itself.

Irrational fears dissolve automatically when we restore the flow of energy and our emotions regain their original meanings as warnings in the here-and-now. There are three aspects to Logosynthesis' work with fears, and you'll now be able to recognise them:

1 An irrational fear is a reaction to an old energy structure that's split off from the energy of the Self

2 This split-off part is entangled with representations of a situation that was experienced as being life-threatening

3 These representations become activated and trigger fear whenever a threat that's similar to the original threat is experienced.

Old fears disappear completely when the frozen structure's energy is moved to where it belongs. Luzia worked with the following three Logosynthesis sentences during our Sunday trip:

1 *I retrieve all my energy bound up in this image of the rock on the road and take it back to the right place in my Self.*

2 *I remove all non-me energy related to the image of the rock on the road from all of my cells, from my body and from my personal space, and I send it to where it truly belongs.*

3 *I retrieve all my energy bound up in all my reactions to this image of the rock on the road and take it back to the right place in my Self.*

The rest of the day was relaxed and our return journey on the narrow road wasn't a problem.

Four starting points for dissolving fear

Luzia's fear was based on a single event in the life of an adult woman. Irrational fears usually have a longer history. If this is the case, you'll generally need to neutralise four types of frozen world. These frozen worlds are listed below (with thanks to Fred Gallo):

1 The *first* experience. The first experience of the fear forms a basic template for the reaction pattern. All other experiences will reinforce this pattern. As soon as the first experience is neutralised, all of the later instances will lose at least some of their distressing characteristics.

2 The *worst* experience. The worst experience cements the reaction pattern. Dissolving the frozen world that exists around this experience removes its sharp edges and supports recovery.

3 The *newest* experience. The most recent experience appears real because of its position so close to our adult consciousness. Working with the newest experience helps to separate the past from the present.

4 The *next anticipated* experience. Memories provide the basis for the belief that the future will be dangerous. There's no difference between memories and fantasies in energy terms; both are thought forms, energy constructs. This is why fantasies are just as powerful as memories when it comes to triggering the above-described biological responses.

Be sure to dissolve the triggers and reactions for these four experiences whenever you apply Logosynthesis to fears.

Contact a trained specialist if you're not confident about working on major issues by yourself. If you do want to dissolve fears by yourself with the help of Logosynthesis, be sure to always employ the following steps:

1 Ensure that you're in a calm and pleasant environment. It's important to feel at ease when you're dealing with fears. If you're uncertain, you can carry out the application together with a trusted other person.

2 Answer meta-question A to establish the symptoms of the fear while you think about only one of the four situations. Also assess the subjective distress that the fear causes you.

3 Answer meta-question B by examining what you perceive when you think about the selected situation. Write down your answer.

4 Formulate the three sentences and say them aloud.

5 Allow the sentences to take effect for a sufficient period. Repeat the relevant sentence if you're distracted during your observation or your thoughts wander.

6 Compare your answers to meta-questions A and B with your new state.

7 End the session or continue with the next aspect.

The following exercise can support you in your work with various fears.

EXERCISE: DISSOLVING FEARS

Create a stack of cards on which are written various activities or events that you fear, e.g.:

- Getting stuck in a lift
- Being locked in a room
- Driving through a long tunnel
- Riding alone in a lift
- Riding in a packed cable car
- Riding a train
- Getting stuck in a piece of clothing with a jammed zip
- Sitting in the back of a two-door car
- Wearing a tight ring on your finger.

Give each activity a number on a 0 to 10 scale of how much it subjectively distresses you, and then order the cards so that the least distressing event is on the top of the stack. We'll begin work on this uppermost topic, so I generally recommend that it has a 6 or less on the distress scale.

Start by asking yourself the meta-questions and then formulate the sentences. You might be afraid of sitting in the back of a two-door car in case the driver has to brake to avoid another car that's approaching from the right. You've assessed this situation as a 6 on the scale. The sentences would then be:

1 *I retrieve all my energy bound up in the experience of sitting in the back seat of a two-door car and take it back to the right place in my Self.*

2 *I remove all non-me energy related to the experience of sitting in the back seat of a two-door car from all of my cells, from my body and from my personal space, and I send it to where it truly belongs.*

3 *I retrieve all my energy bound up in all my reactions to the experience of sitting in the back seat of a two-door car and take it back to the right place in my Self.*

Such sentences are sometimes very long. You can write them down, whether on paper or your laptop screen. Logosynthesis isn't a memory exercise, and the power of the words will still take effect if you read the sentences.

The next aspect

The next aspect can arise within the Logosynthesis work itself, e.g. through you experiencing a physical reaction such as palpitations, pressure in your head, tiredness or dizziness. Drink a glass of water if this occurs. If the symptoms continue, ask yourself meta-question B once more:

If something were to trigger this symptom, where would it be in space?

New sentences will arise from your response. Take a longer break if no new and distressing images or experiences emerge in connection with the topic. Drink another glass of water during this break to support your body with the processing. Then take the next card from the stack.

Don't force anything

Don't force anything when you work with fears. It'd be counterproductive to split yourself into two parts during the Logosynthesis application – one that places you under pressure and the other that's supposed to adapt. This type of courage has no place in Logosynthesis. You can try to climb four stairs at once, but if you want to reach the top of the staircase in once piece, it's far better to take the stairs one at a time.

In general, I don't recommend that you spend more than 40 to 50 minutes each day applying Logosynthesis. You've already had the problem that you're addressing for a long while, so it isn't too important whether the symptoms disappear today or next week. What's critical is that you can live without fear in the long term. Realise that your entire organism has to adjust to a new situation!

Can Logosynthesis make fears worse?

Intense emotions can appear when you begin to work with Logosynthesis. Some people then get the impression that everything is only worsening and so they stop. There are other options.

When you're new to the application of Logosynthesis, you haven't yet experienced how the distressing emotions caused by past experiences are really just energy structures that can be externally activated. It's worth considering every emotion in this way – finding the trigger and applying the sentences. Your contact with your Self will deepen after a while and you'll become less prone to identifying with the old fears. Your conscious ego will initially place you and your emotions on a par with one another, but your Self knows that this isn't the case.

I recommend the involvement of a trained professional if the feelings are too painful and you're not sufficiently confident. He or she can provide you with the necessary security during the processing work.

Chapter 18 in brief:

- Fear is a reaction to fantasies about the course of reality.
- Such fantasies can either match with reality or not.
- If the fantasies match real dangers, people can choose to respond by fighting, fleeing or freezing.
- If the fantasies don't match real dangers, people find themselves in a state of unnecessary stress.
- You can use Logosynthesis to dissolve incorrect fantasies that lead to fears.

19 Overcoming shame

What is shame?

SHAME IS A SPECIAL FORM OF FEAR THAT'S OFTEN ASSOCIATED WITH UNPLEASANT MEETINGS WITH PEOPLE IN EARLY CHILDHOOD. People who feel shame are aware that they've breached a social or cultural norm. Signs of shame include:

- Avoiding eye contact
- Impaired thinking, confusion, loss of direction
- Speech disorders, stammering, stuttering
- Feeling small
- Having a melt-down
- Submission, co-dependency.

In its hidden form, shame can present as boasting and arrogance. Shame is a dissociated state that's connected to strong beliefs and overpowering representations of parental authority. If you feel ashamed, contact with your Essence has been interrupted.

Shame also has a useful side: it helps us to quickly adapt to social rules. It establishes and strengthens our affiliation to our family, group or society.

How does shame arise?

Shame helps you to learn social and societal rules in situations in which you don't yet understand these rules and can't relate to them. This useful process mostly takes place early on in our childhood. But a child's cognitive development often lags behind societal requirements. Why do you have to say 'Thank you'? Why can't you talk with your mouth full? Why can't you walk around without underwear? If parents confront a child with a new infringement and respond by withdrawing their affection, the child is left in a state of confusion that's associated with profound loneliness. This state is what's referred to as shame. A child will often draw irrational conclusions from the parents' irrational behaviour and relate the rejection to his or her own identity. Doing so forms beliefs such as:

– *I'm bad*
– *I don't belong*
– *Something's wrong with me*
– *I'm not loveable.*

Shame can also arise in our adult lives if we enter an unfamiliar cultural environment. I'm still embarrassed when I think back to when I attended an opera in England. During the interval, I went straight up to the bar to order a beer. A woman told me – clearly but with typical English politeness – that English people queued instead of scrambling to the front. I wasn't familiar with this custom because in Holland it's speed and vigour that determine who gets served at bars. The shame struck me straight away and caused me to change my behaviour. I now knew what was expected in England, but if I'd acted in this way in Holland, I'd most likely have died from thirst before I'd ordered my beer!

Shame in everyday life

Shame is an everyday emotion for many people. It's easily activated in many different situations. You take a tub of yoghurt off a supermarket shelf and another tub crashes to the floor, you forget your wedding anniversary, or you serve a vegetarian dinner guest a juicy steak. You're suddenly surrounded by a cacophony of inner voices that consider your action – or even your very being – as wrong, substandard, useless or worthless. The voices repeat old messages from your parents, family members, teachers and classmates.

Shame isn't an emotion that people show gladly. Admitting that you feel ashamed is embarrassing in itself, so people tend to hide their shame and embarrassment. Doing this doesn't lessen the distress and in fact causes cortisol levels in the blood to rise.

The experience of shame activates phrases from our distant pasts as well as images of threatening facial expressions or admonishing postures, e.g.:

- *How dare you act in that way?*
- *Aren't you ashamed?*
- *Put some clothes on!*
- *Don't speak with your mouth full!*
- *You still don't understand!*

Shame and Logosynthesis

Social rules are useful, and you can consciously accept or reject them without feeling ashamed. Shame is a good area for practising your application of Logosynthesis. Remember that it's an emotional reaction to representations of parents, teachers or other representatives of customs and morals. These representations are 'only' energy structures in space and bear hardly any relation to the real people who did their best to raise you as a good member of society.

EXERCISE: DISSOLVING SHAME

The process of dissolving inappropriate shame is made up of the following steps:

- You choose a situation in which you felt or continue to feel ashamed.
- You use meta-question A from Chapter 12 to examine the unpleasant emotions, distressing physical feelings or limiting beliefs that are associated with this situation. These reactions don't only have to be based in shame; feelings of guilt, grief, fear and rage are often also present.
- You give this distress a number on a scale from 0 to 10.

You now look for these reactions' triggers. Shame is a reaction to powerful introjects, and you can only neutralise these introjects if you're aware of them. You'll then be able to make adult decisions about if and how to follow social rules, and without the influence of distressing emotions. Applying Logosynthesis will often reveal how parents were embarrassed by their child's behaviour. The parents' own introjects were activated when their child loudly expressed his or her desire for an ice cream on a crowded terrace. You can find and examine these introjects with the help of meta-question B from Chapter 13. It's best to go straight back to the source of the feeling of shame. If you look back on your life, you'll constantly come across experiences in which parental figures punished you in front of other people for incorrect behaviour. Helpful questions include:

- *From where do I know this feeling?*
- *When have I previously experienced it?*
- *When did I first have this feeling?*
- *Who was present?*

The people who were present on the first occasion will probably have left behind the most important energy traces. Find out where punishing parental figures are in your personal space and how you perceive them.

Where are these figures in space? In front? Behind? To the left? To the right? How far away? How big are they? What are their facial expressions and postures? Answering these questions helps you to precisely determine changes that take place during the course of your Logosynthesis application – even if the emotions don't disappear straight away.

Once you've clarified the details, it's time to apply the Logosynthesis sentences to the scene from your past. If the scene was an image of your mother with a loud and threatening voice, the sentences might be as follows:

1 *I retrieve all my energy bound up in this representation of my mother with this loud, threatening voice saying 'Aren't you ashamed?' and take it back to the right place in my Self.*

> **2** *I remove all of my mother's energy that's related to this representation of her loud, threatening voice saying 'Aren't you ashamed?' from all of my cells, from my body and from my personal space, and I send it to the right place in her Self.*
>
> **3** *I retrieve all my energy bound up in all my reactions to this representation of my mother with this loud, threatening voice saying 'Aren't you ashamed?' and take it back to the right place in my Self.*

Now examine how the distress caused by the embarrassing situation has changed since the start of the exercise on the scale from 0 to 10. Also consider what's happened with your feelings of shame and the associated physical reactions. During the cycle, you may well uncover other events and people that are causing you physical and emotional distress.

I've included a new form of the second sentence in the above example. You can use this form to work with the energy of a single, important reference person.

Shame and beliefs

The previous example saw us neutralise the representation of a reference person in someone's personal space. Doing this is often enough to significantly reduce feelings of shame. If it isn't sufficient, it's important to examine your own beliefs in connection with the presence of shame. What kind of person are you if shame affects you? What beliefs do you have about yourself? You can dissolve these associated beliefs with the help of Chapter 25.

Chapter 19 in brief:

- Shame is the consequence of your confrontation with a broken rule or your reaction to the rejection that comes from having broken a rule.
- Shame plays an important role in the learning of social conventions.
- Shame can lead to distressing beliefs about your own identity.
- Dissolving shame focuses on neutralising representations of important reference people from your childhood.
- Dissolving shame with Logosynthesis allows you to make rational choices about whether you want to comply with social rules.

20 Processing grief

What is grief?

WE GRIEVE WHEN WE LOSE SOMETHING OR SOMEONE:

- Parents, grandparents, relations
- Partners
- Children
- Boyfriends, girlfriends
- Pets
- A job or a career opportunity
- Money
- Goods
- Health.

Grief's natural function is to cause us to pause, withdraw from the world for a while and process the loss. We feel abandoned and we cry. Dealing with loss in a healthy manner involves moving through several phases, from denial of the loss through to grief, anger and depression. This process lets us leave behind our enjoyment of the past and open ourselves up to the opportunities of the present. Healthy grieving sooner or later leads to reassessment – although as the following example demonstrates, this sequence isn't always obvious.

Example: Donna says goodbye

Donna is an attractive artist in her early thirties. She's been together with Vince for quite some time. Vince is a talented, dynamic musician who leads a richly varied life and travels a lot, often taking Donna with him. Their relationship has two sides: it's full of love when the pair get along, but Vince has a short fuse and starts to yell whenever something doesn't suit him. After a fight, he often won't talk to Donna for two days at a time. Donna responds to this silence with self-loathing and grief. Vince is always quick to promise her everything under the sun when he finally comes around. She isn't able to have a calm discussion with him about this pattern. He made a half-hearted attempt to address the issue with a therapist, but this ended without success.

Donna's now turned to me. As we start to talk, it's clear that she's in a state of despair about the relationship. A short while ago she'd been convinced that Vince was the man for her and that he'd change if only she loved him enough. She wants to give the love another chance, but she doesn't really believe that anything will alter. Our session features many elements of the grieving process as it continues:

- Donna despairs that Vince hasn't kept his promise. She needs to give up the belief that he'll change. The topic for the application of Logosynthesis is Donna's energy that's bound up in this belief and her reaction to it.
- Rage emerges once the Logosynthesis cycle is complete. Vince lied to her and manipulated her. The rage is a reaction to the words of his promises and his faithful expression. The application of Logosynthesis is concerned with this awareness.
- Now a fantasy appears – that Vince will soon have new girlfriends if she breaks up with him. This fantasy intensifies her grief. She says the sentences for the fantasy and her grief becomes even more intense. It seems as if she's really facing the reality of the loss.
- Donna realises that the loss isn't just about her relationship with Vince, but also the music scene that fills their shared life. She processes the images of this scene with the sentences.
- We move on to Donna's fantasy of an ideal relationship with Vince. The energy that's bound up in this fantasy is also retrieved. Donna cries for several minutes. The grieving process is really under way.
- The fear now emerges that a new boyfriend has to be a boring boyfriend. Donna takes back her energy from this notion as well.
- When our session comes to an end, Donna reports that she feels better and more relaxed. She says soberly: "It's not going to work with Vince."

Blocked grief

The session with Donna outlines a more-or-less healthy grieving process. She reached the conclusion that her relationship with Vince didn't satisfy her needs and so she set herself on a new course. All of this is easier said than done. Grieving processes are very intense and require considerable time. They appear in many different forms: people can seek out closeness or distance, and many different emotions can take centre stage. It's important to respect any grieving process' individual form, including when you grieve yourself.

A grieving process can become blocked if you keep comparing your current situation with memories of a happier past. This can happen at any point, even after a considerable time has gone by. A blocked grieving process sets you on a constant rollercoaster of emotions with rage, sadness, shame and guilt all alternating over and over again. It's also not just comparing your current situation that can lead to a blocked grieving process. The same can happen with unfulfilled desires, as in the following example.

Example: Jacqueline's ruined plans

Jacqueline is a 71 year-old teacher who was diagnosed with cancer for the third time a year ago. The doctors see her situation as hopeless; she's reached the terminal stage. She seems irate during our session. When I explore this feeling, it turns out that she's imagined leading an 'average' life that ends at 85. She's bound up her life energy in this notion but the cancer has ruined her plans. After a brief discussion, she takes back her energy from this fantasy. What follows is an important phase in which she can cry for the life she desired. She can now turn to the people around her and shape her final days with them in a moving manner.

Grief and Logosynthesis

It doesn't matter whether we're saying goodbye to memories or fantasies when it comes to processing losses with Logosynthesis. Both are categories of constructs that have been created from our own life energy and that of others. Life doesn't abide by our desires but instead plays out in the here-and-now. It's in the here-and-now that we fulfil our mission.

In Logosynthesis, you identify memories of a happier past or fantasies of an unlived life. You take back your energy that's bound up in these memories or fantasies, you remove foreign energy, and you also take back your energy that's bound up in all of your reactions to the remembered or imagined people and situations. You subsequently become able to appreciate full responsibility for your life as it is in the present.

Grieving processes aren't only about being sad. This is just one emotion that can emerge as part of the process. Grief can also mutate into feelings of rage, anger, shame or guilt. A new or slightly different emotion will usually take centre stage after every cycle. Working with the triggers of these emotions is the next step in your work with Logosynthesis.

Traditional counselling models commonly view the emergence of rage in the wake of grief as 'good'. In Logosynthesis, the treatment process doesn't stop with rage. This rage often contains desires and wishes that can't be satisfied. In the end what matters is whether your life energy is really flowing in the here-and-now.

The Logosynthesis approach can sometimes seem rather matter-of-fact – and even cold – when you're dealing with the consequences of losses. If this is the case, realise that the application isn't about the person or beloved object itself, but rather about your energy that's bound up in that person or object. Differentiate between what you've lost and the fantasies and memories that are associated with this loss. If you neutralise these fantasies and memories, you'll be in the here-and-now. Good memories retain an important place in this reality, but you'll also be aware that life goes on.

EXERCISE: LOGOSYNTHESIS AND LETTING GO

- Concentrate on a loss that you've suffered – a relationship, a job, an animal, a place to live or an object.
- Identify your emotions and physical feelings when you think about this loss.
- How great is the distress caused by these emotions and physical feelings on a scale from 0 to 10?
- What representations of the past are associated with this distress?
- What representations of an unlived and impossible alternative are associated with this distress?
- What beliefs are associated with this distress? How could/should your life have been?
- Identify the aspect of a memory or unlived alternative that makes the greatest contribution to the distress.
- Say the Logosynthesis sentences for this aspect.
- Give the sentences long enough to take effect. Find differences from your prior emotions and explore emotions that now emerge.
- Find the new emotions' triggers in the form of memories, fantasies and beliefs. Use these triggers to construct new sentences.
- Take sufficient time for this entire process. You might face many ups and downs, but a new life beckons once everything's complete.

Chapter 20 in brief:

- Every grieving process is individual and contains multiple phases.
- Blocks are possible in every phase.
- These blocks result from frozen memories and unfulfilled desires.
- You only apply Logosynthesis to the energy structures of the memories and unlived alternatives – not to the grief itself.
- The grieving process ends when your life in the present is no longer deprived of any energy.

21 From anger to forgiveness

Beside yourself with rage?

ANGER, RAGE AND FURY ARE EMOTIONS THAT IMPACT OUR COMMUNICATION WITH OTHERS. They're similar to fear from a biological perspective – they're reactions to threats and components of the fight or flight response that takes place in the 'reptilian' part of the brain. Rage and fury are designed to keep our enemies at a distance. Rage also prepares us to use force for the defence of our loved ones, our territory or ourselves.

Rage and fury in their original forms are only of limited use today. In most cases they're entirely inappropriate emotions. Directly expressing rage and fury will normally escalate existing conflicts; acting in these ways rarely leads to a solution.

On a practical level, people tend to see their rage as justified while others find it exaggerated and even destructive. Angry people are often covering up prior hurt and loneliness – experiences and events during which they felt unseen and unappreciated. They behave differently as soon as they notice that their discussion partners are giving serious consideration to their concerns.

Logosynthesis' effects frequently cause people to reassess their situations straight away. They're suddenly able to preserve their own interests without losing sight of their counterparts' needs. You'll no longer be 'beside yourself', whether with rage or otherwise. You'll be you – and in contact with the people who surround you in the here-and-now. The past will cease to become active in the present.

Example: anger in everyday life

Some days are full of opportunities for irritation. I had such a day when I was writing this chapter. My first Skype meeting was scheduled for 8:30, and I left home for my office at 8:15. The trip normally takes eight minutes, but not today; our street was blocked by a delivery van. If its driver had parked correctly, I'd have been able to drive past him before another truck emerged from a building site up ahead and blocked my way again. When I finally reached the next road, I was faced with a small tractor that was chugging forwards on its way to do spraying work in the vineyards. I managed to overtake the tractor but ended up stuck behind two more large vans that were driving infuriatingly slowly.

I made it into my office at 8:30. When I went to my laptop, I found that my assistant had shut it down completely instead of setting it to 'Sleep' mode as I always do myself. I hope that you're someone who can imagine how fuming I was by this point.

When I came to write this chapter later in the day, I realised that what had happened was a typical example of how rage and anger emerge. What had been the problem? It wasn't the other people or the outside world.

The man in the delivery van had given way to the truck driver from the building site. The winemaker and the other van drivers had just been doing their jobs. The real problem was my fantasy of reaching my office within 15 minutes. The tension between fantasy and reality was what led to my anger.

The solution was simple. In the five minutes that it took for my laptop to start up, I formed Logosynthesis sentences for my fantasies that life would obey my wishes and the streets were reserved for me. By the time my client appeared on the screen, the anger was gone.

The old anger

The above example was about anger that arose from a current situation. But our patterns for dealing with anger, rage and fury generally come from our contact with earlier reference people – parents, older siblings and authority figures. These people will have usually expressed their discontent with you or others in a typical way. Two issues may have arisen if you weren't able to process their reactions back then:

- You're frozen in your own past reaction. You react to current situations in a similar way to how you reacted back then – by fleeing or freezing. You activate statues from your personal museum.
- You adopt the patterns of the furious people from your past. Doing this allows you to avoid the original pain and shift its associated harm from your awareness. You now feel, think and behave like your reference people.

EXERCISE: DISSOLVING ANGER

You have a reason to apply Logosynthesis as soon as your anger begins to harm you and other people. Search for the original trigger for your current anger by asking yourself the following question:

Who made me angry back before I was able to defend myself?

When you know who's providing the model for your anger, examine exactly where this person is within your personal space. Then say the sentences:

1 *I retrieve all my energy bound up in (the image, voice or energy of the old reference person) and take it back to the right place in my Self.*

2 *I remove all non-me energy related to (the image, voice or energy of the old reference person) from all of my cells, from my body and from my personal space, and I send it to where it truly belongs.*

3 *I retrieve all my energy bound up in all my reactions to (the image, voice or energy of the old reference person) and take it back to the right place in my Self.*

Now examine how the representation of the reference person has changed.

Anger in the brain

People who are familiar with Logosynthesis often report that completing just one such cycle makes it much easier to think about a situation that previously made them angry. This isn't surprising, as anger that's based on a frozen pattern activates the amygdala in the brain and causes you to respond by fighting, fleeing or freezing. It doesn't matter whether the frozen pattern is your own or a pattern that you've adopted from someone else. When you react in this way, the brain reduces the blood flow to its higher centres and limits your ability for rational thought.

Many emotions associated with past events no longer have any function. They're like broken vinyl records that keep playing the same sound. Dissolve these patterns, regardless of how justified they may appear. Freedom in the here-and-now results from energy in flow – energy that was bound up in history and fantasy before this point.

Forgiveness

When you retrieve your energy from old constructs and your reactions to these constructs, you also decide to forgive. This isn't just an act of charity: it's an act of cleansing your energy system. The energy that's bound up in your reactions to someone else's actions goes back to that other person. Your own, new path is free.

In Logosynthesis, there's no basic difference between repressing or expressing rage and anger. We split off parts of our life energy in both cases, and both patterns inhibit contact with our Essence. Good health, satisfying work and loving relationships are only possible when our energy flows freely.

Forgiveness frees you from the narrow limits of the past and re-establishes your connection to your Essence, to the living Self. It also creates better conditions for the future than rage and anger. The following exercise helps you to forgive.

EXERCISE: ANGER AND FORGIVENESS

- Imagine approaching someone who's hurt you.
- Use meta-question A to explore your emotions and physical feelings when you think about this person.
- Now use meta-question B to examine where the triggers for these emotions and physical feelings are – in space or your body. Say the three sentences for these triggers.
- Open yourself up to all of the fantasies that you associate with the person. The desire to send him or her far, far away may well be the most innocent. Form and say three sentences for the energy that's bound up in these fantasies.
- Consider what you've lost as a result of the person's actions. Form and say three sentences for the energy that's bound up in the representation of these losses.
- Consider all of your expectations of the person – how he or she should behave or should have behaved. Form and say three sentences for the energy that's bound up in these expectations.
- Consider all of your expectations of yourself in the situation when you were hurt. Form and say three sentences for the energy that's bound up in these expectations.

This exercise can help you to reassess the situation and free your energy. If you don't feel relaxed and balanced after you've completed the exercise, you haven't dealt with all aspects of the harm that the person caused.

The experiences that you address in the exercise may also have even older painful experiences lying beneath them. Take the time to uncover these earlier experiences and perform the above procedure again.

Chapter 21 in brief:

- From a biological perspective, anger exists to defend our boundaries from people and animals with bad intentions.
- This evolutionary strategy was useful in the past, but it doesn't make much sense in our highly evolved culture.
- We adopt our models for expressing anger, rage and fury from the people who showed these emotions towards us when we were young.
- Logosynthesis can neutralise old representations of people and scenes.
- This neutralisation helps us to express our discontent more effectively or accept a situation's inevitability.

22 Unleashing love

> **It is not good for Man to be alone.**
> -- THE BIBLE, GENESIS

Relationships

RELATIONSHIPS HAVE DIFFERENT BIOLOGICAL AND PSYCHOLOGICAL FUNCTIONS. These functions are partly opposed to one another, and people live in a constant dilemma between stability and change. If there's too much stability then we're bored, but if there's too little stability then we're unsettled. This makes relationships very vulnerable to dissociative mechanisms. Living, developing relationships exist only in the here-and-now. Frozen worlds inhibit the real perception of all of our counterparts.

Between one third and one half of all first marriages currently end in divorce. You might expect partners to learn from their experiences, in turn improving the chances for second marriages. But people prefer changing their partners to changing their patterns of thought, feeling and behaviour. These people aren't really present in the here-and-now with their current partners. They're instead activating patterns that lead to failed or stalled relationships.

I've found six disturbing relationship patterns in my work with Logosynthesis:

1. Transference
2. Trauma
3. Longing
4. Desires
5. Idealisation
6. Fear

These patterns generally appear in combination and are directly connected with frozen worlds from the past. There are many opportunities for their activation every day, whether or not you're currently in a relationship.

The patterns inhibit both the development of your current relationship and the leaving behind of relationships that have ended. You also block your entry into new ways of life that could provide you with increased satisfaction. All parties involved are then prevented from fulfilling their life's task.

1. Transference

The other person is unconsciously confused with someone else. Many spouses see one another through the image of their own mother or father. A man tends to confuse his partner with his mother and a woman expects her husband to react like her father. It's worthwhile taking back your energy from these old parental images and returning your parents' energy to them.

2. Trauma

Harm and insult are caused in all relationships if partners neglect or ignore the other person's needs – whether consciously or subconsciously. Significant or unexpected harm and insult can leave traces in your energy system. These traces become triggers for reactions of rage, disappointment and abandonment that are always the same.

It's worthwhile neutralising such frozen recollections instead of confirming them. The quality of your relationship will improve if you can perceive your partner in the here-and-now instead of through the lenses of the past.

3. Longing

Idealisation occurs at the start of every relationship as you magnify strengths and mask weaknesses. In contrast, everyday life in a healthy relationship sees the partners learn to deal with one another and develop realistic perspectives. The relationship freezes if this learning and development fails, and longing then begins for the days that are over. If you bind up life energy in ideals, you'll tend to give up your relationship instead of these ideals.

The idealised memory of the partner stands in the way of a live encounter with the partner in the present. The application of Logosynthesis removes the bound up energy from this memory. The energy then becomes available for the development of the relationship.

This notion may seem paradoxical at first glance. Why should you neutralise such a wonderful image? The answer is simple: the partner in the image no longer exists, and comparing your partner with this romantic ideal will frustrate both sides. Logosynthesis works from this idea. You apply it by identifying a memory that triggers nostalgic feelings and then saying the sentences:

1 *I retrieve all my energy bound up in this wonderful memory of my partner and take it back to the right place in my Self.*

2 *I remove all non-me energy related to this wonderful memory of my partner from all of my cells, from my body and from my personal space, and I send it to where it truly belongs.*

3 *I retrieve all my energy bound up in all my reactions to this wonderful memory of my partner and take it back to the right place in my Self.*

Remember that it's the bound up energy that's the problem, and not the energy that flows in the here-and-now.

4. Desires

Lovers anticipate their partners' wishes and satisfy these desires in the (secret) hope of having their own deepest desires satisfied. Later, during everyday life, they discover that they've been short-changed by their adjustment. The partners then need to talk. There are two approaches for applying Logosynthesis in this situation:

- You explore your fantasies of what could happen if you stopped anticipating your partner's desires
- You explore and process what you need from your partner.

Bound up energy blocks development in the present in both cases. Everything becomes possible when this energy flows.

5. Idealisation

My good friend Carlotta once said: 'Love is seeing the other person as God meant him.' This is nicely put, but it only works in contact with Essence. Idealisation of a partner distorts our view of our own Essence. The experience of profound happiness is connected with the partner's character or presence, which in turn leads to dependency. We end up jumping out of the frying pan and into the fire.

It seems paradoxical to take back energy from representations of loved ones. What we're actually interested in is the energy that's bound up in these images. If your partner really is ideal, he or she will remain so even when your energy is flowing! Use the following sentences to take back the energy:

1 *I retrieve all my energy bound up in this ideal image of my partner and take it back to the right place in my Self.*

2 *I remove all non-me energy related to this ideal image of my partner from all of my cells, from my body and from my personal space, and I send it to where it truly belongs.*

3 *I retrieve all my energy bound up in all my reactions to this ideal image of my partner and take it back to the right place in my Self.*

6. Fear

Many people fear losing their partner through divorce or death. They imagine how they'd stay lonely and helpless. They ignore their own Essence and give up their power and strength.

If you're bothered by such fears, I recommend that you treat them with Logosynthesis as is covered in Chapter 18. It's true that you may have to say goodbye to a loved one at some point, but everyone will be better off if you live in the present and don't bind up your energy in distressing future scenarios.

Logosynthesis in relationships

In working with relationships, Logosynthesis sometimes triggers resistance due to its pragmatic attitude to the restoration of contact with the energy flow of Essence. It would be incorrect to assume that this attitude leads to egotism; the Self always meets others in the here-and-now, and there's a deep awareness that we're all connected, all of the time.

Logosynthesis sometimes conflicts with the romantic ideal that people should put themselves out or even make sacrifices to make one another happy. In practice the reverse is true. When we dissolve frozen memories, fantasies and beliefs about a relationship, we come to see the man or woman behind them in the here-and-now. This man or woman will be much more attractive than a frozen image ever could be. Nevertheless, doing this also means that you have to take responsibility for your own behaviour in the here-and-now; you can no longer pass off this responsibility to anyone else.

When you apply Logosynthesis, you become the creator or your own happiness in the very truest sense. And what happens when you take on this role? Your partner will generally start to create alongside you. But you may also have a blinding realisation: you've actually married your mother or father, or you've spent years cultivating unrealistic expectations that your partner will never be able to fulfil. Working on a relationship between two people is never easy for a variety of reasons:

- The relationship seldom really takes place in the here-and-now. The personal space of both partners is occupied by introjects of parents, siblings and prior relationships – all supported by religious, political and societal authority figures. These introjects trigger reactions that blur each partner's view of the other person in the present.
- Relationships activate very early dependency patterns. This makes it difficult to discuss relationships openly.
- Our culture makes high demands of relationships as sources of happiness, diversion and stability. This culture is expressed in films, songs and varied self-help literature.

- Relationships are governed by a subtle balance of power. The process of change can shake up this balance and cause significant uncertainty for both sides.

You should therefore approach relationship issues with caution, always giving your partner a real chance to react to your changes.

Example: Peter reassesses his marriage

Peter is a 40 year-old social worker who took part in a Logosynthesis course. During the course, he described how he felt restricted in his relationship with his wife, Marianne, and how his obligations as a father and family breadwinner were robbing him of happiness. He longed for a life in which he was only responsible for himself. The couple's sex life had been on hold for years and there were barely any hugs and kisses any more, either. Peter has come to see me because of an affair that he's had with a colleague's wife that's threatening to plunge him into serious trouble.

When I examine his motivation for the single life more closely, it quickly becomes clear that he harbours a desire for tenderness and sex with another woman. He describes his relationship with Marianne as a 'corset' – caused by many grievances and misunderstandings that have occurred during twelve years of marriage, ten of which have been with children. Several non-marital relationships have damaged communication between the pair. The current liaison has also led to a serious confrontation in which Marianne has made it clear that she's ready to discuss the relationship's future. Peter appreciates this but feels at least some delight at the prospect of becoming involved with another partner; too much damage has already been done.

Peter's use of the word 'corset' sticks out in our conversation like a sore thumb. Another topic is his fantasy of being able to find exactly the devotion and tenderness with another woman that no longer seems available in his relationship with Marianne. He's created an inner picture of Marianne as a bitter, cold and distant woman. In contrast, the 'unknown alternative' is sexy and affectionate – even though she doesn't exist. I give Peter the following sentence:

I retrieve all my energy bound up in this corset and take it back to the right place in my Self.

Peter relaxes considerably and a loving smile appears on his face. I ask him what he now perceives. He describes how he sees Marianne, how her bitterness has dissolved and how she now seems open to him. He also remembers how she'd once said that he couldn't really see her. It's only now that he understands what she'd meant.

We proceed to work on taking back the energy from Peter's notions of being alone and the 'unknown alternative.' I also let him return Marianne's energy to her from his body and personal space. As we end the session, he says: "That's better now. I can talk to her at last. I don't know what will happen, but it'll be exciting to find out."

Developing through relationships

Do you want to reshape your life? If so, your relationship with your partner provides the very best practice ground. It offers abundant material, day after day. It's not a problem for your learning if you don't have a partner at this point. You can still neutralise memories from the past as well as expectations of future relationships. Your chances of finding success in a future relationship will then increase.

Don't try to neutralise all of your accumulated patterns in one go. Instead deal with them step by step. Work with aspects or individual situations rather than entire people. Dissolve frozen images of romantic dream relationships, idealised honeymoons and raw break-ups. Your partner will end up treasuring you all the more as a result.

EXERCISE: CLARIFYING A RELATIONSHIP

Conflicts occur in every relationship. Some of these conflicts will be big while others will be small. Think back to a situation when you were unhappy with a partner:

- *Who was it?*
- *What was the conflict about?*
- *Where did the conflict take place?*
- *How did you behave?*
- *How did your partner behave?*
- *How did you feel at the end?*
- *How significant is the distress caused by these feelings now on a scale from 0 to 10?*

Next answer meta-question B:

- *Where do you perceive your partner in space if you think back to the situation? Left? Right? In front of you? Behind you? Above you? Below you? How far away?*
- *How do you know that this representation is there? Do you see it? Hear it? Feel it?*

Now place a chair in the location where you perceive your partner to be in your memory of the conflict. Take your own seat once more and make a brief note of your emotions, bodily sensations, and distress on a scale from 0 to 10. Then say the following sentences:

1 *I retrieve all my energy bound up in the representation of X in this conflict and take it back to the right place in my Self.*

2 *I remove all non-me energy related to the representation of X in this conflict from all of my cells, from my body and from my personal space, and I send it to where it truly belongs.*

> **3** *I retrieve all my energy bound up in all my reactions to the representation of X in this conflict and take it back to the right place in my Self.*

Allow the sentences to take effect and then look for changes in your perception of your partner and your reaction to this perception. Is the person still in the same place? Is it still about the same topic? Begin another cycle if you find that new topics have emerged about everyday relationship issues.

Relationships in perpetual flow

It's counterintuitive from a romantic perspective to take back your energy from experiences and images of loved ones and and return their energy to them. But relationships occur in the here-and-now and they can't advance if you bind up energy in an ideal.

If you currently live alone and fail to say goodbye to a past relationship, you deprive yourself and your possible future partner of a chance at development – and so also of a chance at happiness.

Applying Logosynthesis opens up a new perspective on you, your Self and your life. You don't have to hurt as much as the split-off part makes you inclined to accept. Quite the opposite, in fact: when you've applied Logosynthesis, you'll finally be able to see where relationship potential exists within your life.

Bring awareness of your Essence into your relationship. Doing so is contagious; many relationships start from a shared experience of Essence, and this experience is always sleeping under the surface, ready to be awoken.

Chapter 22 in brief:

- Relationships are only partly lived in the here-and-now.
- Emotions, memories, fantasies, desires, beliefs, societal rules and the partners' distressing experiences with one another all stand in the way of dealing with reality as it is.
- Logosynthesis dissolves these factors' effects and establishes clarity.
- Space is then opened up for direct contact between the partners – or for an amicable separation.

23 Revitalising the body

The body between Essence and the world

OUR BODY IS AN INTERESTING PHENOMENON. It's the intermediary between our Essence and our earthly environment. We only perceive that which reaches us via its senses, and we rely on its help to move through three-dimensional space. We don't notice it for the most part; it's a loyal servant behind the scenes. We can enjoy the body as a source of pleasure and positive experiences, whether through our well-being, physical performance or sex. We can also see it as a hindrance if it doesn't work alongside us to fulfil our tasks and satisfy our desires.

Highest pleasure and deepest pain are therefore closely connected with our experiences of our bodies. An extreme mountaineer who climbs steep rock faces without ropes relies on the strength and skill of his fingers and toes and applies his total concentration on his way to the peak. Tennis players such as Roger Federer, Novak Djokovic and Rafael Nadal achieve perfection on the court. Lovers enjoy their union with all of their senses, and a foodie relishes all seven courses of a luxurious meal.

On the other hand, there's no escaping the fact that the body isn't perfect. We grow up and experience our physical prime, but it's downhill from there in terms of beauty, strength, skill and speed. At the end of the descent, everyone faces death. The body only exists as a perfect machine for a certain part of life, and even then not for everyone. Sooner or later we're all confronted with symptoms of decline, whether acute or chronic. Life is limited and the body is finite.

Perspectives on the body

Our perception of the body depends on how we see the world, e.g.:

- The body is a machine in the service of my goals. Craftsmen, sportsmen and soldiers tend to see the body this way, and I'm consciously listing men here. Injuries or limitations are repaired with chemicals or technical manipulation.
- The body is given to me by fate and provides me with challenges. I can struggle against fate or make the best out of what occurs.
- The body is my window to the world. It allows me to share what happens around me and react to these events.
- The body is a manifested energy structure and obeys the same laws as all other energy forms.
- The body is an instrument of my indestructible Essence.

Your perspective on the body will influence the way in which you handle its symptoms and faults.

Logosynthesis and the body

There are several aspects to applying Logosynthesis to bodily symptoms:

1. A physiological or functional symptom itself
2. The degree to which the symptom interferes with your life
3. Your knowledge and beliefs about the symptoms and your treatment options
4. Frozen energy structures in connection with emotional distress.

All of these aspects affect the development of the symptoms and their healing.

1. The physiological or functional symptom

Suffering is only partly determined by its symptoms. I often wondered about the differences between patients that I observed during my work at an alpine clinic for people with chronic lung conditions. A young man who could climb the highest mountain in the area suffered horribly from relatively minor complaints. He compared himself with healthy men of his age. On the other hand, an old woman was proud of being able to climb the stairs up to the building's third floor by herself, and was glad to enjoy the fascinating mountain panorama from her window. Physical symptoms don't need to determine the way you live your life.

2. The degree of interference

The extent to which a physical symptom interferes with your well-being isn't solely dependent on your body. Context also plays a role. A secretary whose eye disease means that she can no longer work at a computer faces different problems from a mother of young children who has exactly the same symptoms. The secretary needs to retrain professionally, but the mother can continue to fulfil her educational role with only minor inconvenience.

The degree of interference equally depends on whether the impairment leads to loss or grief. A motorcyclist whose accident means that he can no longer do his job or take part in his favourite sport will suffer more than someone who can continue their love of painting pictures after being involved in the same accident.

3. Knowledge of symptoms and their treatment

Knowledge of symptoms and their treatment can affect you in two ways:

- Knowledge can help you to handle symptoms. You know what you have to do to minimise the condition's consequences, whether in a crisis situation or everyday life. Treating chronic lung conditions or diabetes is much simpler if patients are informed about their illness and how it's being treated. They'll take medicines more regularly if they have a better understanding of what these medicines do.

– Information about symptoms can lead to blocking fantasies about the illness' course and the options for treatment. Even the first mention of a cancer diagnosis can be lethal for some people.

4. Energy structures and their effect on the body

Staying healthy requires the body to be able to interact freely with its environment. You may have an energy structure of your father in the top-left of your personal space, for instance. He's constantly encouraging you to work hard, and this isn't a problem in itself. But does this representation continue to push when you've done enough? Your health can be affected if the message is repeated out of context time and time again.

Old images in your personal space can trigger grief, anger, rage or resentment and cause distress. You end up poisoning and punishing yourself if someone has disappointed or hurt you and you allow an energy construct of that person to remain in your space. The other person doesn't even know that you're keeping this image or that it bothers you.

Representations of distressing situations can weaken your immune system and make you susceptible to illness. The life energy that's bound up in frozen energy structures is no longer available for healing.

Healing energy flows

Logosynthesis doesn't pretend to be able to heal the body. It's no replacement for conventional or complementary medical treatment. It can nevertheless relieve suffering by initiating a process that allows you to perceive your body and its symptoms in a different way.

This altered perception can help you to adjust your requirements to your body, give up damaging habits, and consider new treatment possibilities. Working with Logosynthesis lets you neutralise troublesome energy structures and your reactions to these structures.

Your body can then become a clear and open vessel for the Self – a vehicle for your task in the Earth Life System as described in Chapter 4. Your life energy can flow without obstruction when your body, mind and Essence are in harmony. When the distress from the symptoms decreases, healing will become easier.

Emotions and physical symptoms

Physical suffering is often closely associated with emotions such as fear, shame, guilt, anger, disgust and grief. These emotions don't just affect the bearer of the physical symptom, but also those around him or her.

Emotional suffering generally feels just as bad as physical suffering. It can sometimes feel even worse. A good starting point for applying Logosynthesis can therefore be to retrieve the energy that's bound up in symptoms. Bound up energy blocks healing, so it's better if no energy is frozen in old parts.

Here's an example from my own life. A few years ago I spent several months suffering from a lung disease that medicine had difficulty treating. It was very cold, so I couldn't leave our house for the entire time. This restriction would doubtlessly have led to impatience and dissatisfaction during an earlier phase in my life. But now the self-application of Logosynthesis allowed me to remain almost completely calm, as per the idea:

Everything that is may be.

I used my unexpected house arrest to write and prepare my lectures and seminars for the coming year. I remained calm at all times. The illness ended up getting better more quickly than I'd expected because all of my energy was available for my healing.

The past in the present

Physical suffering can reactivate other, older losses and injuries. If someone suffers from an illness that caused significant distresses for the people around them during their childhood, this person probably retains the worries, irritations and disappointments of others as energy structures. This applies in particular to chronic illnesses that require large-scale lifestyle adjustments from both the affected person and his or her relatives. Emotions can therefore be active in both one person and others.

Beliefs and physical symptoms

Physical symptoms aren't just connected with strong emotions, but with numerous beliefs as well. These beliefs are also present as energy structures. They can be conclusions that are based on life experiences or convictions that are copied from messages received from others in the environment.

When we're ill and don't understand our situation, we tend to accept the first interpretation that's given by the people around us without posing further questions. Statements from doctors, parents, family members and friends receive an influence that doesn't always match up with those people's levels of knowledge.

Apply Logosynthesis to beliefs about your body and illness in the same way that you'd treat any other belief. You start out with the symptoms' characteristics and their potential for change. There are almost no unshakeable truths about illnesses and treatments. Many ideas about these matters are determined by energy structures that are never questioned:

- *Cancer can't be healed*
- *Everyone in our family is overweight and diets don't work for us*
- *Asthma is inherited; you can't do anything about it.*

Treatment options change and medicine changes with them. Stomach ulcers are no longer seen as a symptom of stress, but rather as an infection of *helicobacter pylori*. Cancer therapy has made enormous progress, and ideas about the consumption of eggs, red wine, chocolate and coffee change every second weekend.

Beliefs contain frozen worlds, and you can use Logosynthesis to neutralise these worlds. You can then reorient yourself with open eyes and ears.

Logosynthesis and physical symptoms

Applying Logosynthesis to physical symptoms always makes sense. There are various approaches:

- The physical symptoms themselves and your reactions to them are topics for the content of the sentences. This approach offers immediate relief because it's not usually the symptoms that distress us, but rather what we bind up in our thoughts and feelings about these symptoms. When Logosynthesis is applied regularly, we see that life energy begins to flow once more and natural healing processes are accelerated. A woman who had suffered from serious dizzy spells for years became symptom free after just two Logosynthesis sessions.

- The body can stand in the way of our planning. We have to put up with limits or realise that the body might want to tell us something important about our lifestyle. Logosynthesis helps to clarify physical limits. Jacqueline, the cancer patient from Chapter 20, came to realise that fighting the cancer was now less important than meeting her friends on positive terms. She said her goodbyes in a moving and meaningful manner.

- Many frozen messages from the outside world are bound up with serious illnesses. Diagnoses, treatment methods and medicines are often not just appreciated as facts; they're highly charged with personal and societal beliefs. A radiologist once examined one of my friends and told her: 'Get your affairs in order.' When the tumour later turned out to be benign, this message had been frozen into her energy system and disappeared only when she applied Logosynthesis.

- Physical objects or phenomena can also form introjects. This may seem strange, but it's especially important for applying Logosynthesis to allergies and post-surgery pains.

Examples of non-human energy structures

At a seminar in a small group, an older participant, Joachim, worked to dissolve the consequences of a traffic accident that he'd been involved in three years ago. He addressed the image of the car speeding towards him as he walked, the screeching of the brakes, and the panic that he was about to be run over.

He was relieved once he'd dissolved these aspects of the trauma, and he subsequently went on to say how he'd also like to get rid of the pain in his leg. He'd had this pain since being hit by the car's bumper. I gave him the following sentences:

1 *I retrieve all my energy bound up in this representation of the car's bumper and take it back to the right place in my Self.*

2 *I remove all non-me energy related to this representation of the car's bumper from all of my cells, from my body and from my personal space, and I send it to where it truly belongs.*

3 *I retrieve all my energy bound up in all my reactions to this representation of the car's bumper and take it back to the right place in my Self.*

It was an experiment that immediately resulted in success, as the pain that Joachim had suffered from for three years disappeared within two minutes. Two weeks later, I received an email from him thanking me for the seminar. The pain never returned.

Joachim's incident with the car bumper isn't the only example of dealing with a non-human representation from the outside world. Ingrid, a 45 year-old participant at one of my seminars, suffered from continual pain after abdominal surgery that she'd had ten years ago. I gave her three sentences to address the energy representations of the surgeon's hands and tools. Her inner organs began to move as soon as she paused for the sentences to take effect. This movement continued through the night. By the next day the pain had disappeared and her belly felt warm and alive. This result remained over the long term.

I've also profited from such applications myself. When I caught a cold during a summer trip in a car with the air conditioning turned up too high, I applied Logosynthesis to remove the energy representations of the cool flow of air. I stopped sneezing within minutes.

Allergies

Allergies are a special field of application for Logosynthesis because they appear to follow its basic principles exactly. If you have hay fever, your immune system interprets harmless pollen as being dangerous. Your entire body then enters into a state of high alert as soon as spring descends. Your eyes and nose actively try to remove the invaders, but it's all a false alarm because the pollen isn't actually harmful. The representation of the pollen is simply programmed as harmful and your body reacts accordingly.

The solution to the problem seems unbelievable, but all it involves is a simple and consistent application of Logosynthesis' principles.

EXERCISE: HAY FEVER

Take a break as soon as you notice the first signs of hay fever in the pollen season – sneezing, itchy and running eyes, and reddening of the skin. Find 20 minutes to sit down somewhere quiet and say the following sentences for the pollen that's just appeared:

1 *I retrieve all my energy bound up in the representation of this pollen in my immune system and take it back to the right place in my Self.*

2 *I remove all non-me energy related to the representation of this pollen in my immune system from all of my cells, from my body and from my personal space, and I send it to where it truly belongs.*

3 *I retrieve all my energy bound up in all my reactions to the representation of this pollen in my immune system and take it back to the right place in my Self.*

Repeat these sentences at different times and in different places. I've been symptom-free as a result of Logosynthesis for several years, although I had to use the sentences again last spring while I enjoyed a ristretto on a railway station terrace in Milan. The blossoming trees in the city were foreign to my immune system, so my body triggered its old defences once more.

Logosynthesis doesn't promise healing

Logosynthesis offers a broad palette of possibilities for overcoming physical symptoms and complaints. I'm often asked if it would be possible to do away with medical care as a result of its effects. I generally recommend that Logosynthesis is only used to complement and support necessary medical care, and not to replace it. When the flow of life energy is disturbed, it generally takes years for physical complaints to become apparent. It's then rather uncommon for the consequences of this process to be reversed in just a few sessions. The realignment of energy that's required to heal physical symptoms can take days, weeks or months to materialise, and that's if healing is possible at all.

Chapter 23 in brief:

- The body is an interface between Essence and the world.
- Disturbances in our connection to Essence can show up as physical symptoms.
- Beliefs about the progression of illnesses and their treatment can disturb healing.
- You can apply Logosynthesis to emotional distress and limiting beliefs that arise from physical symptoms.
- Logosynthesis is also efficient at neutralising allergies and long-term side effects of accidents and operations.
- Logosynthesis can support medical care but doesn't make it unnecessary.

24 Kicking habits

Habit and addiction

WE'RE SUPPOSED TO STOP SMOKING, EAT LESS, DO MORE SPORT AND WATCH LESS TELEVISION. We all have our habits – or better yet, our habits have us. Do you want to know what someone will do tomorrow? It's simple: look at what they're doing today. It's 99 per cent certain that they'll do the same when tomorrow comes around.

The desire to kick our habits creeps up from time to time. We make good resolutions on New Year's Eve or our birthdays, but then we continue to act as before. Only when our suffering increases are we motivated to change; the smoker's cough starts to hurt or the weight shown on the scales becomes alarming. Nevertheless, we fail in our attempts if our Essence is left out in the cold. Bad habits generally have split-off parts and introjects:

- Split-off parts stabilise our view of the world as helpless slaves to habit. Bad habits mostly emerge as 'solutions' – to repress the pain of deep childhood trauma, to reduce stress or to avoid responsibility. Young people smoke because the want to belong. The nicotine biologically reduces stress and increases social bonds. Adults drink because they find it difficult to spend time with other people. Such habits help with 'state management.' They help us to counter life's challenges. Smoking, eating and drinking also welcome us into a more pleasant state. This state doesn't last for long, but we can extend it by indulging in more of the same with the pull of a corkscrew or the push of a button. The habits therefore have the benefit of providing positive emotions and the drawback of causing us long-term harm.

- Introjects take up the opposite position. We're all familiar with past messages from our personal space that start out, 'You should…' We're confronted with obvious disadvantages via messages on packets such as

'Smoking kills', via bans and via reduced career opportunities for alcoholics and the obese. Such introjects can be activated at certain times of the year, with good intentions perhaps being put forward at New Year. A doctor may equally activate representations of parental figures; a third of smokers give up when their doctors directly tell them to do so.

Old representations of the outside world are permanently fighting with the split-off parts. They normally lose because helpless people simply can't be forced to act in any particular way.

The fight between the two types of energy structures can't be won with psychology. The opponents are both well-practised and well-matched. The split parts deny the long-term damage of habits, and limiting beliefs confirm habits if insight into their damage absolutely can't be avoided:

- *I won't manage to give up*
- *It's like the devil's work; something always goes wrong when I want to give up*
- *It's as if I'm being controlled from afar*
- *I can't change my drinking habits.*

Bad habits are bound up with intense and constant emotions. Guilt and shame make us feel bad, while relaxation from cigarettes and serenity from intoxication raise our spirits. For a moment it feels good to stuff yourself with a couple of Big Macs at McDonalds.

Example: Paul gives up smoking

Paul is a participant at one of my seminars. When he wants to go outside to smoke during one of the breaks, I ask him if he wants to give up the cigarettes. He says that he does, but adds that he's already tried without success on many occasions. I ask him why he smokes. He says, "Sometimes I want a cigarette, and sometimes I just can't do without one." I ask him how he knows that it's now time for a cigarette. He replies that he doesn't exactly know. When I ask him what happens in his body in the 30 seconds before he lights up, he notices a pulling feeling around his sternum. I ask him if he'd still want to smoke if this pulling feeling wasn't there.

He's surprised at this thought and answers, "No." Now I begin to explore the roots of the pulling feeling. You'd expect it to be linked to his desire for a cigarette, but when he goes back in time, he discovers that he knew the feeling long before he'd first smoked. I go further back in time with him and he uncovers a memory in which his parents left him at home and he had to wait for them to return all by himself.

Loneliness was also a topic for him during puberty, and when he became friendly with a group of young people who smoked, it was obvious to him to smoke as well. He then learnt that old feelings of loneliness disappeared with the nicotine flash that was offered by a cigarette. Over time he came to confuse the cause with the effect – eventually assuming that the pulling feeling in his chest meant that he needed a cigarette.

We now have enough material to begin a Logosynthesis application. He processes the memory of his parents leaving him and the similar experience of loneliness during puberty. When we finish, the pulling feeling disappears. Paul stops smoking straight away.

Logosynthesis and bad habits

Paul's story shows how habits begin:

- There are physical and emotional reactions to distressing events, generally from early childhood. Parental figures are unable to recognise or satisfy the child's need for security, respect and protection. These events cause the child's contact with his or her own Essence to be broken off because the necessary security is missing.
- The memories of these events are so painful that the person wants to avoid bringing them to the surface.
- The person learns that the memories are less painful when he or she takes certain substances or behaves in a certain way.
- Consuming certain substances (sugar, alcohol, cannabis, tobacco etc.) or acting in a certain way (working, racing, playing sport, gambling etc.) becomes a habit.

- As time goes by, the pain of the memories comes to be understood as a trigger for the avoidance habit. The distressing memories are no longer accessible.

Paul's story also shows how you can dissolve habits:

- You identify physical signals that prompt you to consume the substance or pave the way for the avoidance behaviour.
- You go back in time and find events during which you first felt these physical signals.
- You neutralise the signals' triggers with the help of Logosynthesis.

'Positive' beliefs about bad habits

One of Logosynthesis' special applications is to target 'positive' beliefs that are connected with damaging behaviour. You don't just have to neutralise the effect of distressing experiences, but also the beliefs that sustain the fallacy that a habit is something good.

An aspect of bad habits is how people do something that harms them over the long term so as to enjoy a good feeling in the short term. Examples include alcoholics who have one more drink to feel better, motorists who try to drive at 100mph down the motorway to boost their adrenaline levels, and the shopaholic stocks trader who takes home the newest designer piece in every single colour.

All of these people get a good feeling from a damaging behaviour, albeit only for a few minutes. These 'positive' emotions are bound up with beliefs that deny the damaging effects of the habit or substance:

- *It's good for me to smoke from time to time*
- *Almost everything in the world is already banned – it's good to drive super fast now and again!*
- *People who can't enjoy a good meal are boring*
- *Life becomes a little easier when I drink.*

The following chapter shows you how to directly dissolve such beliefs.

EXERCISE: HABITS

- Concentrate on a habit that you want to give up.
- Examine your pattern for this habit. How often do you do it? How does it start? How does it continue? How do you end it?
- Find out how you physically react to the fantasy of giving up the habit.
- Find out how you emotionally react to this idea.
- How great is the distress about this idea on a scale from 0 to 10?
- Go back in time and look for the moment when you first reacted to a person or event with this physical sensation or emotion.
- Examine the representation of this person or event with the help of meta-question B.
- Repeat the procedure for everything that comes up until you're able to imagine giving up the habit without feeling any distress.
- Give up the habit and apply Logosynthesis to all troubling fantasies, memories and beliefs that emerge over the next few weeks and months.

Connections with other applications

Draw on the other chapters in Part IV whenever you apply Logosynthesis to damaging habits. You can question entire sets of beliefs – arguments that justify a pattern but can't stand up to critical analysis. Distress is sure to emerge when you give up familiar behaviour patterns; shame, rage and fury will appear, all entangled with old triggers.

You won't usually give up damaging habits from one moment to the next. You'll first have to neutralise as many aspects as it takes for your Self to acquire at least 51 per cent of the decision-making authority. The awareness that your true Self isn't suffering makes habits and addictions less powerful.

Chapter 24 in brief:

- Bad habits arise from the avoidance of pain after previous hurt.
- When you work with Logosynthesis, you identify key events and neutralise representations of past people and incidents.
- You can neutralise all beliefs that support your habits with the help of Chapter 25.
- You'll then feel less pressure to suppress your physical and emotional reactions to the representations with the help of habits.

25 Dismantling beliefs

> Whether you think you can
> or you think you can't:
> you're right!
>
> -- HENRY FORD

Beliefs

LOGOSYNTHESIS RESTORES THE FLOW OF ENERGY BETWEEN ESSENCE AND THE WORLD AROUND US. We can focus its application on thoughts, feelings and actions that are connected with a topic that directly bothers us – or we can use it to address underlying beliefs and fundamental convictions.

Our thoughts, actions and even our emotions all emerge on the basis of beliefs. Whoever believes that the world is a place for learning can approach other people without fear. But whoever believes that others are after him or her is sure to behave in a fearful, aggressive or defensive manner.

Beliefs define our inner and outer reality. They help us to find our way in life without having to reorient ourselves on a daily basis. This is a much more efficient method than daily reorientation, as our brains require three times more energy to process new information than they do to process familiar information.

How do beliefs emerge?

Beliefs emerge when people have to process new events but only have limited information available. We form many convictions during childhood that we don't question; we're quickly overwhelmed and our brains aren't yet able to process complex information. This particularly applies when we're between four and six years old, the age at which we enter society. We're faced with two options in these situations:

1. We assume others' convictions without questioning these convictions. Our parents' beliefs simply become ours. If Luca's father is afraid of dogs and tells Luca, "Watch out! Dogs bite!", his son doesn't have many facts available. He can't know that some dogs are dangerous while others aren't. His father's authority leads Luca directly into the belief that all of these creatures are dangerous. He'll then avoid dogs in future and his father's belief will never be explored.

2. We draw our own conclusions from our experiences of the world. Our brains aren't yet fully developed, so this information will be limited or distorted. Consider a mother who's expecting important guests and is busy preparing a delicate soufflé. Five year-old Sarah comes into the kitchen and wants to show her mother her new drawing. Her mother screams, "Not now! Can't you see that I'm cooking?" Sarah places this rejection on her own shoulders and assumes that something's wrong with her. Such one-sided conclusions are limiting, but they're still more reassuring than living a life without any understanding at all.

Beliefs become more stable with age, and they eventually turn into our frames of reference. They can then either simplify or complicate our lives. Some beliefs also emerge when we're adults, as the following example from Rebecca makes clear.

Example: Rebecca applies Logosynthesis to a belief

Working with beliefs can sometimes help us to overcome blocks in our application of Logosynthesis. 63 year-old Rebecca has successfully learnt to apply Logosynthesis for herself, but one day she encounters a problem. She tells me about her fear that her son will be imprisoned. This fear comes up every time she reads about a robbery, murder or rape in the newspaper. She fantasises that her 40 year-old son has committed these crimes and she sees images of him behind bars. She's tried to apply Logosynthesis to this issue on several occasions, but something's gone wrong on every attempt.

When she introduces this topic in one of our sessions, the belief behind both her fear and the prison fantasy becomes clear: 'My son is a potential criminal.'

I ask her where this belief is located in her personal space, and she replies, "Across the entire width of the room, above me." She then pauses for a moment and says, "It's a guillotine… hanging over me," before starting to cry. She now applies the sentences, using the guillotine as a topic. As we go through the first cycle, the guillotine turns into an old-style parchment that's rolled up at both ends. There's a barely readable phrase printed on the sheet. After the second cycle, the parchment starts falling apart. When she removes the foreign energy from the parchment with the second sentence of the third cycle, a strong force pushes it far away and over the mountains.

During this process, the belief that her son is a criminal disappears – along with the fear that he might commit a crime.

Beliefs and change

If you want to change something in your life, you'll often find that an endless series of blocking convictions stands in your way. We'll restrict ourselves to the most limiting beliefs here, i.e. those that relate to the impossibility of change.

My colleague Fred Gallo identified a series of special beliefs and convictions as part of his work on energy psychology. These beliefs and convictions can sabotage or hinder changes for the better. They have the following themes:

- Feasibility
- Deserving
- Identity
- Money
- Will
- Right
- Risk
- Worthiness
- Loss
- Time

Feasibility

I can't solve this problem.

You believe that you don't have the competency, ability or skill to change the situation.

Will

I don't want to solve this problem.

You expect other people to solve the problem because they have more resources available. But you're the person who's actually suffering.

Worthiness

I'm not worthy of solving this problem.

You believe that your personal significance isn't sufficiently great. A part of you devalues yourself and therefore you don't make efforts to solve the problem.

Deserving

I don't deserve to solve this problem.

A part of you believes that you're not sufficiently accomplished or haven't tried sufficiently hard to solve the problem.

Right

I don't have the right to solve this problem.

A part of you believes that you don't have the right to take on a task even though other people don't seize the initiative to find a solution.

Loss

I'll lose something if I solve this problem.

A frozen part of you believes that you'll lose something important.

Identity

This problem is a part of me.

You fear losing your identity, but you don't yet know that an identity based on your Essence will free you from all fear.

Risk

It's dangerous for me to solve this problem.

A part of you is afraid of new things and you're unaware of resources that will become available to you once you start something new.

Time

I don't have time to solve this problem.

You're not convinced of the importance of solving the problem. All other activities are currently more important.

Money

I don't have the money to solve this problem.

All other expenses are more important than solving the problem. Like lack of time, lack of money says something about your priorities.

You can sabotage many changes with the limiting beliefs listed above. They bind up energy and lock you into a downwards spiral. It then becomes more difficult to recognise and seize opportunities for positive change. The following exercise helps you to identify limiting beliefs when it comes to solving problems.

EXERCISE: BELIEFS

Concentrate on an everyday issue that's bothered you. What happened? Who was there? What was it about? Find out which beliefs from Fred Gallo's list are valid for you with regard to this problem.

I use a scale from 0 to 10 to assess a belief's level of truth – just like the scale that's used to determine the subjective level of distress. On this new scale, a 0 means that a belief is entirely false or completely irrelevant, while a 10 means that you're absolutely convinced by its content. Give a number to each of the beliefs in the following list and then order them according to their level of truth. Here's the list once more:

- *I can't solve this problem*
- *I don't want to solve this problem*
- *I'm not worthy of solving this problem*
- *I don't deserve to solve this problem*
- *I don't have the right to solve this problem*
- *I'll lose something if I solve this problem*
- *This problem is a part of me*
- *It's dangerous for me to solve this problem*
- *I don't have the time to solve this problem*
- *I don't have the money to solve this problem.*

Other beliefs

The beliefs listed here are just some of many. It's worthwhile investigating this matter further, as you can prevent many problems by dissolving limiting beliefs. The search isn't easy, of course. Limiting beliefs lie underneath everyday thoughts and feelings and are rarely expressed directly. Uncovering them requires detective work. The key question is always:

If a belief were to cause this problem, what would that belief be?

If you're annoyed because a rival has taken your dream job, for instance, you might ask yourself:

1 *What do I believe about myself?*
2 *What do I believe about others?*
3 *What do I believe about life?*

Possible answers:

1 *I'm a loser*
2 *Others always manage to win*
3 *Life's unfair!*

These beliefs damage your self-confidence and your career if you feed them. Find out how long you've already believed them and how you arrived at them. They probably have very little to do with your colleagues.

Applying Logosynthesis to beliefs

Beliefs are bound up with old representations of the outside world and your reactions to these representations. You can apply Logosynthesis as soon as you identify a belief or memory, regardless of its content. All limiting beliefs are just energy constructs that have lost connection with the here-and-now and your Self. The Logosynthesis sentences release these energy constructs.

You can dismantle limiting beliefs with the following steps:

- Find a situation, a feeling, a thought or a behaviour pattern that bothers you.
- Find the most important belief that's associated with this topic and write it down.
- Find out how valid this limiting belief is on a scale from 0 to 10. 0 means 'Entirely false' or 'Irrelevant', while 10 means that you're absolutely convinced.

- Find the belief's location within your body or personal space by asking yourself the following questions:
    - *Where is the belief in space or my body?*
    - *In front? Behind? To the left? To the right? Above? Below?*
    - *How do I know that the belief is there?*
    - *Do I see an image or can I hear a voice in my body or personal space?*
- The next step is to say the Logosynthesis sentences:

1 *I retrieve all my energy bound up in the representation of this belief (X) and take it back to the right place in my Self.*

2 *I remove all non-me energy related to the representation of this belief (X) from all of my cells, from my body and from my personal space, and I send it to where it truly belongs.*

3 *I retrieve all my energy bound up in all my reactions to the representation of this belief (X) and take it back to the right place in my Self.*

- Always allow enough time for the sentences to take effect.

Then reassess the processed belief's level of truth on the 0 to 10 scale and consider the changes that have occurred. Examine the belief's position in space, its form or voice, its wording, and your reaction to it.

There are many layers in the application of Logosynthesis to limiting beliefs. Keep at it!

Deeper work with limiting beliefs

The application of Logosynthesis that's described here considers limiting beliefs to be independent energy structures in space. Once you've identified a limiting belief that you want to change, assess its truth on the scale from 0 to 10. Then find its location in space or within your body, examine how it appears to you as an image or a voice, and set the Logosynthesis sentences to work. There are two possibilities for going a step further:

- You examine from whom the relevant limiting belief comes. Who told you this about yourself or the world? Was it your father, your mother, a teacher, a priest or a doctor? Then apply the Logosynthesis sentences to the belief's original owner – starting from this person's representation within your personal space.

— You find out whether the limiting belief was a conclusion that you reached in reaction to a situation that bothered you as a child. Did you overwhelm your parents on a bad day, and did they then reject you without putting this into words? If so, apply Logosynthesis directly to the situation that led you to your earlier conclusion.

Chapter 25 in brief:

- Emotions, physical symptoms, thoughts and behaviours are based on deeper beliefs.
- These beliefs can limit our potential.
- We can apply Logosynthesis to these limiting beliefs.
- We treat them as if they were independent energy constructs.
- We can also neutralise past situations that have led to limiting beliefs.

PART V
IN CONCLUSION

Final thoughts

EVERYONE'S LIFE STORY CONTAINS MANY UNPROCESSED EVENTS. The topics are different and the Logosynthesis sentences have different effects – but if you apply Logosynthesis on a regular basis, the iceberg of unprocessed experiences will slowly begin to melt.

Humans aren't perfect, and they don't need to be. The human consciousness can only process information at a rate of 40 bits per second, but the world around us throws some 40 million bits of information towards us each second. You'll therefore experience many incomprehensible and inconceivable events even as an adult. You'll experience so many of these events, in fact, that you'll continue to split off new parts and have your energy stored in frozen representations of your environment long into your old age. It's not surprising that monks withdraw from the world and spend many years meditating so as to find enlightenment; there are simply too many challenges on the path to wholeness. This means that a lot of material emerges on a daily basis to which Logosynthesis can be applied. It's a form of psychological cleansing for small, unspoken irritations and for the fact that a perfect world doesn't and never will exist. With time, Logosynthesis can become like brushing your teeth – for your soul.

You don't have to do it alone

You can process many topics with Logosynthesis by yourself, but sometimes it's better to rely on the support of a trained professional. Examples of such situations include when:

- You want to learn how to apply Logosynthesis on yourself but with someone else's support. The specialist will be a coach, teaching you how to use the method.
- You're doing well on an everyday basis, but you need support for processing particular experiences – especially traumatic events from childhood. A specialist can help you to activate and then neutralise these topics.
- You have troublesome physical or emotional symptoms that aren't covered in this book or are too painful or distressing to process alone. A trained psychotherapist will be able to provide you with assistance.

Want to know more?

The Logosynthesis International Association continues to develop and spread Logosynthesis across the globe. It maintains the www.logosynthesis.net website in various languages for the benefit of the public, Logosynthesis practitioners and training institutes. The website lists recognised specialists and features a wealth of articles and support materials.

Those interested in applying Logosynthesis as a professional coach, counsellor or psychotherapist can also visit the website for information on the requirements and training programme.

Bibliography

Almaas, Ali Hameed (1998). *Essence With the Elixir of Enlightenment: The Diamond Approach to Inner Realization.* Weiser Books.

Assagioli, Roberto (2000). *Psychosynthesis: A Collection of Basic Writings.* Synthesis Center.

Berne, Eric (1961). *Transactional Analysis in Psychotherapy.* New York: Grove.

Bucay, Jorge (2005). *The Power of Self-Dependence: Allowing Yourself to Live Life on Your Own Terms.* Harper Paperbacks.

Callahan, Roger (1985). *Five Minute Phobia Cure: Dr. Callahan's Treatment for Fears, Phobias and Self-Sabotage.* Enterprise Publishing, Inc.

Craig, Gary (2008). Emotional Freedom T*echniques.* URL: www.emofree.com.

Frankl, Viktor E. (2000). *Man's search for ultimate meaning.* Perseus Pub.

Gallo, Fred (2005). *Energy Psychology. Explorations at the Interface of Energy, Cognition, Behavior and Health.* Boca Raton, FL: CRC Press.

Grof, Stanislas (1998): Human Nature and the Nature of Reality: Conceptual Challenges from Consciousness Research. *Journal of Psychoactive Drugs,* Vol. 30, No. 4.

Hell, Daniel (2002). *Die Sprache der Seele verstehen. Die Wüstenväter als Therapeuten.* Freiburg: Herder Spektrum.

Kafka, Franz (1966). *Betrachtungen über Sünde, Leid, Hoffnung und den wahren Weg.* Frankfurt am Main: Suhrkamp.

Lammers, Willem und Kircher Beate (Eds.) (2002). *The Energy Odyssey. New Directions in Energy Psychology.* Maienfeld: ias Verlag.

Lammers, Willem (2008). *Logosynthesis – Change through the Magic of Words.* Maienfeld: ias Verlag.

Lammers, Willem (2009). *Phrases to Freedom.* Creative Space.

Morschitzky, Hans (2009). Angststörungen. Diagnostik, Konzepte, Therapie, Selbsthilfe. Vienna: Springer.

Patanjali (1997). *Yoga Sutras.* Translated by Alfred Scheepers. Amsterdam: Olive Press.

Shapiro, Francine (2001). *Eye Movement Desensitization & Reprocessing. Basic Principles, Protocols and Procedures.* New York: Guildford Press.

Sharma, N.V. (1963). Indische Erziehung. *Pädagogische Rundschau, Monatsschrift für Erziehung und Unterricht,* (10). Ratingen. Alois Henn Verlag.

Tart, Charles T. (2007). What Death Tells us about Life. *Shift at the Frontiers of Consciousness,* November issue, p. 30-35.

Wilber, Ken (2000). *A Theory of Everything. An Integral Vision for Business, Politics, Science and Spirituality.* Boston: Shambhala.

About the author

WILLEM LAMMERS, DPSYCH, MSC, TSTA IS A SEASONED SPECIALIST IN THE SUBTLE NUANCES OF MIND, BODY AND SOUL. He gathered a broad range of experiences as a coach, psychotherapist, trainer and executive at the VU University in Amsterdam and an alpine clinic in Davos before going on to found *ias*, an institute for the instruction of specialists in guided change. He trained in transactional analysis, hypnotherapy, NLP and energy psychology and organised Europe's first energy psychology conference in 2001. He has devoted himself to developing and spreading Logosynthesis since 2005. Dr. Lammers now shares his expertise as a coach, psychotherapist, author, seminar leader, speaker and Logosynthesis trainer, primarily in Europe and North America. This is his fifth book.

Disclaimer

THE INFORMATION CONTAINED IN THIS BOOK IS EDUCATIONAL IN NATURE AND IS PROVIDED ONLY AS GENERAL INFORMATION FOR PERSONAL USE. The author accepts no responsibility or liability whatsoever for the use or misuse of the book's information. Please seek professional advice as appropriate before implementing any protocol or opinion expressed in the book and before making any health-related decisions.

Logosynthesis is a relatively new approach and the extent of its effectiveness, benefits and risks is not fully known. The reader agrees to assume and accept full responsibility for any and all risks associated with reading this book and using Logosynthesis as a result.

The reader understands that if he or she chooses to use Logosynthesis, emotional or physical sensations or additional unresolved memories may surface which could be perceived as negative side effects. Emotional material may also continue to surface after Logosynthesis has been used. This surfacing indicates that other issues may need to be addressed, preferably with the help of a trained professional. Previously vivid or traumatic memories may equally fade when Logosynthesis is used. This fading could adversely impact your ability to provide detailed legal testimony regarding a traumatic incident.

Logosynthesis is not a substitute for medical or psychological treatment. The information presented in this book is not intended to imply the use of Logosynthesis to diagnose, treat, cure or prevent any disease or psychological disorder. The author makes no warranty, guarantee or prediction regarding any outcome for using Logosynthesis for any particular issue. The case reports presented in this book similarly do not constitute a warranty, guarantee or prediction regarding the outcome of an individual using Logosynthesis for any particular issue.

You need to become sufficiently trained and qualified as a Logosynthesis practitioner in order to use Logosynthesis with others.

While all materials and links to other resources are included in the book in good faith, the accuracy, validity, effectiveness, completeness or usefulness of any information contained herein, as with any publication, cannot be guaranteed.

If any court of law rules any part of this Disclaimer to be invalid, the Disclaimer stands as if those parts were struck out. By continuing to read this book you agree to all of the above.

Made in the USA
Charleston, SC
04 November 2016